# Anton Edelmann's
# CHRISTMAS
## FEAST

# *Anton Edelmann's*
# CHRISTMAS
## FEAST

Traditional festivities – Food, Fine Wines and
Frivolities – from The Savoy's Maître Chef

TED SMART

**Author's Acknowledgements**
I would like to thank the Directors and Management of The Savoy, especially
Mr Ramon Pajares and Mr Duncan Palmer for their support during the writing
of this book.
Warm thanks and appreciation to the HarperCollins team, Barbara Dixon who kept smiling,
no matter what, and Heather Thomas.
But nothing good is ever achieved without the enthusiasm of The Savoy kitchen team and my thanks
to them for sharing this essential quality in abundance and for their dedication and hard work.
I also thank all the colleagues and friends who helped me with this book, particularly Derek Rooke and
Nana Yaw Ntiri-Akuffo for helping with the writing of recipes, and Jaxson Keedwell who tested them.
My thanks also to Laurence Beere for selecting the superb wines, and to Peter Dorelli for the wonderful cocktails.
To my secretary, Sophia Petrides, and Barbara Levy, thanks for their continuous support and last, but very
far from least, my wife Sue, for her tremendous understanding.

A TED SMART Publication 1996
First published in 1996 by HarperCollins*Publishers* London
Text © 1996 Anton Edelmann
Photographs © 1996 HarperCollins*Publishers*

A catalogue record for this book is available from the British Library.

ISBN 0 583 32631 5

For HarperCollins*Publishers*
Editorial Director: Polly Powell
Commissioning Editor: Barbara Dixon
Production: Bridget Scanlon

Designed and produced by SP Creative Design
147 Kings Road, Bury St Edmunds, Suffolk IP33 3DJ
Editor: Heather Thomas
Designers: Al Rockall and Rolando Ugolini
Recipe testing: Penny Marland

Flower arrangements by Fleur de Lys, Bury St Edmunds

**Photography**
Photographer: Steve Lee
Home economist: Kerenza Harries

Colour reproduction by Saxon Photolitho, Norwich, UK
Printed and bound by Rotolito Lombarda S.p.A., Italy

# CONTENTS

# INTRODUCTION

The magic of Christmas comes from many different things, not least of which is the wonderful food we eat at this special time of year. Naturally, you would expect a chef to say this – and you are quite right!

However, it is unimaginable to think of Christmas without traditional food and drinks. The smell of freshly baked Christmas cake, the scent of hot mulled wine infused with fruit and spices, the aromas of roast turkey, goose or pheasant with apple or bread stuffing, mingling with the distinctive smell of the fir tree. These are pleasures that we all remember from our childhood.

Many of our favourite seasonal recipes have evolved over many centuries from regional peasant food. However, in recent years, a vast range of dishes and ingredients from all over the world have made a big impact on our kitchens. The earthy, robust flavours of the Mediterranean, and cous-cous from North Africa; the intense aromatic spices and herbs of the Far East; and the turkey itself, which hails from the New World, have all added to our Christmas repertoire. The choice of fresh produce from all over the world, which is now available in our supermarkets, delicatessens and specialist shops, is truly dazzling.

Our perception of what constitutes the perfect Christmas feast has altered in another way: the increased emphasis on healthy eating. This is not a condemnation of plum pudding, mince pies and chestnut stuffing, which all have their place on the traditional table. It is simply a recognition that lighter food and simpler ingredients have their part to play.

A similar change has taken place in our attitude to alcohol. The new range of wines and liqueurs from the New World has brought exciting alternatives to more traditional drinks, and these are well worth exploring. But remember that non-alcoholic drinks and cocktails can be equally delicious and a more sensible option if you have to drive.

For me, the most abiding memory of Christmas comes from my childhood. We lived at the foot of the Alps. Sometimes Christmas was white, whereas sometimes an early snow would melt leaving the lower slopes of the mountains bare. The countdown to Christmas began with the Advent Kranz my mother baked, filling the house with a rich and wonderful smell.

Before dinner on Christmas Eve, my family made a 'magic punch' of wine, rum, sugar and spice. The intense aroma of my father's punch, the shadows thrown by the lights of the tree and the carols we sang, dressed in our Sunday best, signalled that Christmas had truly begun.

After opening our presents on Christmas Eve we sat down to a sumptuous dinner which began with marinated salmon served with a sweet mustard dip and some home-made blinis, or marinated herring fillets in sour cream with sliced apple and chives, served with boiled potatoes.

Next would be roast pheasant, wild duck or pot-roasted leg of venison. The main course was always always accompanied by home-made spätzle (a pasta speciality of the region), carrots and Brussels sprouts with roasted chestnuts. My father, on excellent form having partaken of several glasses of wine, maintained that a leg of venison had more flavour than a saddle, but Mother said that buying the less expensive leg joint was nothing but meanness! A teetotaller, she even disapproved of drinking at Christmas.

Dessert was warm rumtopf served with cinnamon ice cream and home-made biscuits or lebkuchen. My mother's aversion to alcohol did not extend to this – her speciality and her pride and joy. In the larder, she kept an earthenware pot filled with sugar and rum. As the summer slowly ripened the soft fruit in our garden, freshly picked strawberries, raspberries, blueberries, blackberries, plums, mirabelles and cherries were added to the pot in turn, layer by layer. By the time Christmas arrived, the long slow marination had soaked the fruit in sugar and rum. Heated gently, this wonderful ghost of summer provided welcome insulation against the bitter weather of mid winter.

The climax of Christmas Eve was walking through the cold to midnight mass. Christmas Day itself was for visiting. Friends, relatives and neighbours came to see us

– and to sample Mother's irresistible rumtopf. On Boxing Day, we ate a salad followed by traditional roast goose with plum and apple stuffing, and potato dumplings with braised red cabbage. The meal ended with a dessert of home-made ice cream and warm cherries.

At The Savoy, over the festive period, the public rooms are beautifully decorated, and in the Front Hall a magnificent Norwegian fir tree is ablaze with thousands of tiny white lights. The Savoy provides a calm oasis of luxury and stylish relaxation after the pressures of work and the bustle of Christmas shopping. However, behind the calm exterior, everything is hard work and ceaseless activity. By mid-October, our reservations book for Christmas and New Year's Eve is full. Preparations for the six-course Christmas Day lunch are well under way.

With the arrival of Christmas, chestnuts are peeled and glazed; stuffings are mixed; stocks are prepared and reduced to sauces; fish is filleted and packed between layers of ice; Christmas cakes and logs are iced and decorated; turkeys and geese are dressed and roasted; thousands of mince pies are baked; and Christmas Puddings are flambéed in a sea of brandy.

Beyond the kitchen door, the restaurant looks fabulous and there is a terrific atmosphere. The tables are crowded with families: parents, children and their grandparents. I always greet as many of our regular customers as possible. When the first table is served, the kitchen settles down into a rhythm and I return from the restaurant to help with the starters. Halfway through, I run down to the pastry chef to check the puddings and the champagne sauce. The whole brigade helps with the hot fish course, an ambitious dish demanding last-minute preparation but one that always looks and tastes superb and is well worth the effort.

Soup is served and then on to turkey, beef or goose with Brussels sprouts, glazed chestnuts, Belgian endives, small roast potatoes and button onions. I ask myself how can they eat so much? Then I remember that it's Christmas.

The telephone rings and it's my wife. Our turkey is cooking well in the oven at home but she has dropped the gravy and there aren't enough Brussels sprouts for our twelve guests. I tell her that I will buy some from The Savoy. Sometimes it pays to be a chef.

By now all the main dishes have been served and the brigade starts clearing up. We all help to send out the puddings, mince pies, chocolate logs and Christmas cakes. At about three o'clock, the battle has been won and we can safely hand over to Father Christmas who makes his traditional visit to the restaurant every year.

One of the secrets of successful cooking is planning ahead. That's why, as the guests linger over their coffee and petits fours, I sit down with the impressions of the day still fresh in my mind and write the menu for next year's Christmas.

In the evening, the restaurant is closed and I am on my way home with emergency supplies of extra gravy and Brussels sprouts. When I step through the front door, Christmas begins all over again. I put on my apron and take over from my wife who has been what she calls 'turkey sitting'.

We have about twelve guests for Christmas dinner – smoked salmon parcels with salmon trout, roast turkey with chestnut stuffing, Brussels sprouts and glazed chestnuts. There's a haunting familiarity but if it's good enough for The Savoy, then it's good enough for my own table at home.

Our pudding is supplied by Mrs Wood, an old friend of the family who has eaten with us every year. Everyone agrees that she makes the best Christmas pudding in the world.

Please don't be daunted by any of the recipes in this book, particularly ones that appear to be complex and long. I have tried hard to keep them simple and well within the range of any enthusiastic amateur cook. As well as Christmas Day, there are recipes for Christmas Eve, Boxing Day, New Year's Eve and even a festive vegetarian menu. Be adventurous and try them, and have a very happy Christmas.

# ANTON EDELMANN'S
# TOP TEN CHRISTMAS TIPS

A successful Christmas begins early with good planning. To give you an idea of how early this should be, I always write my Christmas and New Year's Eve menus the previous Christmas and New Year when the memories and festive atmosphere are still fresh in my mind and I can experience the seasonal spirit all around me. Once you have selected your menus, you can work out a timetable and countdown, and, hey presto, before long it will be Christmas again.

## 1 Plan your menus carefully
■ Take care not to repeat textures, colours, cooking and preparation methods.
■ Have a good balance of hot and cold, savoury and sweet, and a choice of dishes, such as meat, fish, salads, vegetarian options and brunch.
■ Take into account the nutritional value plus all the modern considerations about health and the calorie content of food.
■ Think about presentation and how you are going to serve the meal.
■ Try and spread the workload to avoid last-minute rushing and panics.
■ Sometimes, after a rich and heavy meal on Christmas Day or New Year's Eve, it's a good idea to prepare something light and simple for the following day.

## 2 The Christmas pudding
Prepare the Christmas pudding in July or August, and remember to soak the fruit for two weeks, so that it can swell and give the pudding plenty of moisture.

## 3 Mince pies
These can be made in October and then frozen until the holiday period. Again, the mincemeat should be mixed two weeks before you use it to fill the pies.

## 4 Christmas cakes
Traditional Christmas cake and stollen should be made

by mid-November. Leave the cakes to dry out for ten to twelve days before putting on the marzipan and icing. You may wish to make the cake even earlier and 'feed' it with brandy, rum or liqueur for several weeks before decorating it. Wrap the stollen well and leave to mature before eating it.

## 5 Cook what you need

A common mistake is to buy too much food and cook more than you need. There is nothing worse than a surfeit of leftovers which nobody feels like eating. People do not eat a lot more at Christmas than they do during the rest of the year – they just think they do. If there are only three or four of you, perhaps you should opt for a turkey breast instead of a huge turkey or goose.

## 6 Keep it simple

Don't make unnecessary work for yourself. Order all your food quite early from your butcher and fishmonger. Be very precise in your ordering, i.e. the weight, and how it should be cut and prepared. It will save you a lot of time, for no extra cost.

## 7 Seasonal sauces

A good Christmas requires a good sauce, so put aside a few hours about a week before Christmas to prepare the sauces and store them in screwtop jars or in the freezer.

## 8 Vegetables

Prepare all the vegetables for Christmas lunch the day before, so that all you need do on the day is to cook them, and relax with your family and guests.

## 9 Decorating the house

Purchase the Christmas tree and decorate the house before you start your food preparation – you cannot do everything at once.

## 10 Learn to delegate

Last, but not least, delegate some of the work and make sure that everyone is involved in the preparation and that they all work harder than you! You will have more time then to enjoy the festive season.

# SEASONAL STARTERS

In the following pages, you will find a delicious array of first courses, featuring fish, shellfish, meat, salads and vegetarian dishes. They are all relatively easy to make when you are busy entertaining and have little time for cooking complicated meals. And when you need a light and refreshing way to start a meal before a rich main course, these recipes will inspire you.

# EGG PANCAKES *with* CRAB

This is a delicious way to start a festive meal. The delicate crab meat contrasts
with the rich sweetness of the egg pancake.

### SERVES 4

*200 ml (7 fl oz) mayonnaise*
*100 ml (3¹/₂ fl oz) tomato ketchup*
*10 g (¹/₃ oz) grated fresh horseradish*
*100 ml (3¹/₂ fl oz) natural yogurt*
*50 ml (2 fl oz) orange juice*
*2 teaspoons chopped fresh chives*
*dash of Tabasco*
*115 g (4 oz) white crab meat*
*50 g (2 oz) smoked salmon, cut in julienne strips*
*3 plum tomatoes, skinned, seeded and diced*
*8 medium eggs*
*2 tablespoons chopped fresh herbs, e.g. chervil and tarragon*
*40 g (1¹/₂ oz) unsalted butter*
*assorted salad leaves, to garnish*
*salt and freshly ground black pepper*

***For the salad dressing:***
*1 teaspoon Dijon mustard*
*1 tablespoon white wine vinegar*
*4 tablespoons olive oil*
*pinch of caster sugar*
*salt and freshly ground black pepper*

**1** Mix together the mayonnaise, tomato ketchup, horseradish, yogurt and orange juice. Add the chives and season to taste with salt and pepper and Tabasco.

**2** Mix the crab meat with the smoked salmon and tomato, and stir in a spoonful of the prepared mayonnaise sauce.

**3** Beat the eggs and herbs with some salt and pepper. Heat a little of the butter in a small frying pan and pour in a little of the egg pancake mixture. Swirl around the base of the pan and then cook over low heat until the pancake is set and golden underneath. Turn over and cook the other side. Keep warm while you cook the remaining seven pancakes in the same way.

**4** Divide the crab filling between the pancakes and fold each one in half. Make the salad dressing by stirring all the ingredients together and use to toss the salad leaves. Arrange some salad on each serving plate. Place two filled pancakes on each plate and pour a little of the remaining sauce over the top.

**Wine:** *Riesling Kabinett, Rheinpfalz 1992 (Germany)*

# CARPACCIO OF SALMON *and* BRILL

This recipe could not be simpler, and it can be prepared up to one week in advance. The distinctive flavour of the pesto sauce infuses beautifully into the fish.

### SERVES 4-6

*1 x 400 g (14 oz) long piece of salmon fillet (cut from one side of the fish and skin and bones removed)*
*400 ml (14 fl oz) Light Pesto Sauce (see page 90)*
*150 g (5 oz) fillet of brill, all skin and bones removed*
*115 g (4 oz) mixed salad leaves, e.g. curly endive, lamb's lettuce, oak leaves, rocket*
*salt and freshly ground black pepper*

### For the dressing:
*4 tablespoons olive oil and 1 tablespoon lemon juice*
*salt and pepper*

1 Cut the fillet of salmon along the centre to open up like a butterfly. Spread a spoonful of pesto sauce on half of the salmon lengthways. Place the fillet of brill on top, and then spread with another spoonful of pesto. Fold the other half of the salmon over the top.

2 Wrap the salmon and brill 'parcel' in cling film and freeze until required – up to one week, if wished.

3 When ready to serve, defrost and unwrap the salmon and cut into thin slices, 1 mm (¹/₁₆ in) thick. Arrange the slices, overlapping each other, around the edge of each serving plate.

4 Mix the olive oil, lemon juice and seasoning together to make the dressing, and mix in the salad leaves. Add some freshly ground black pepper and arrange the salad in the centre of each plate. Grind a little more pepper over the fish and dribble with a little pesto sauce.

**Wine:** *Laurent Perrier, Brut N. V. (Champagne)*

## CHEESE PUFFS
### MAKES 30

*40 g (1¹/₂ oz) unsalted butter*
*115 ml (4 fl oz) milk*
*¹/₄ teaspoon salt*
*65 g (2¹/₂ oz) plain flour, sifted*
*2 eggs, beaten*
*50 g (2 oz) Manchego cheese, grated*
*4 tablespoons pine kernels*
*¹/₂ teaspoon Dijon mustard*
*oil for deep frying*
*paprika for dusting*

1 Bring the butter, milk and salt to the boil. Off the heat, beat in the flour. Beat in the eggs, a little at a time, then stir in the cheese, pine kernels and mustard.

2 Heat the oil and deep fry teaspoonfuls of the cheese mixture over medium heat for about 5 minutes, until crisp. Drain and dust with paprika.

# ROMILLY'S STUFFED CRAB CLAW SALAD

This dish is influenced by the flavours of the Far East. It could be topped with other shellfish, fish, chicken or quail as an alternative to crab.

SERVES 4

200 g (7 oz) white crab meat
1/2 tablespoon finely chopped fresh root ginger
1 red chilli, seeded and finely chopped
25 g (1 oz) frozen prawns, squeezed and finely chopped
1 tablespoon cornflour
2 eggs, beaten
3 tablespoons white breadcrumbs
vegetable oil for deep frying
1/2 garlic clove, crushed
2 spring onions, chopped
1 tablespoon sugar
2 tablespoons sesame oil
1/2 teaspoon red wine vinegar
2 tablespoons light soya sauce
juice of 1/2 lime
2 tablespoons chopped fresh coriander
100 g (31/2 oz) mangetout, cut into julienne strips and blanched
100 g (31/2 oz) cucumber, peeled and cubed
100 g (31/2 oz) vermicelli, cooked and refreshed
1/2 tablespoon sesame seeds
salt and pepper

1 Mix the crab meat with half the ginger, half the chilli and the prawns. Season with salt and pepper. Sprinkle mixture with a little of the cornflour and then shape into four 'crab claws'.

2 Sprinkle the 'claws' with the remaining cornflour, dip into the beaten egg and then coat with breadcrumbs. Deep fry in oil at 180°C, 350°F until golden brown. Remove from the oil and place on absorbent kitchen paper. Keep warm.

3 Mix the remaining ginger and chilli with the garlic, spring onion, sugar, sesame oil, red wine vinegar, soya sauce, lime juice and coriander. Mix with the prepared mangetout, cucumber and vermicelli, and arrange in the centre of four serving plates. Top with the deep-fried 'crab claws' and sprinkle with sesame seeds.

**Wine:** *Sauvignon Blanc, Santa Monica 1993 (Chile)*

# FRANCESCA'S LAMB *and* PEPPER RAGOUT

Pasta! Who can exist without it? This makes a good supper dish or is perfect for the day after the
feasting and excesses of Christmas Day or New Year's Eve.

## SERVES 4-6

*150 g (5 oz) fillet of shoulder of lamb, minced*
*2 eggs, beaten*
*40 g (1¹/2 oz) breadcrumbs*
*40 g (1¹/2 oz) carrot, diced*
*100 g (3¹/2 oz) onion, diced*
*40 g (1¹/2 oz) celery, diced*
*2 garlic cloves, crushed*
*100 ml (3¹/2 fl oz) olive oil*
*400 ml (14 fl oz) vegetable or chicken stock*
*2 bay leaves*
*200 g (7 oz) tomatoes, skinned and diced*
*450 g (1 lb) macaroni*
*75 g (3 oz) red pepper, seeded and sliced*
*75 g (3 oz) yellow pepper, seeded and sliced*
*a few basil leaves, chopped*
*salt and pepper*

**1** Mix together the minced lamb, beaten egg and
breadcrumbs. Season with salt and pepper, and then
roll into 1.5-cm (³/4-in) balls.

**2** Cook the carrot, onion, celery and garlic in some of
the olive oil until the onions are soft and translucent.
Add a little vegetable or chicken stock and the bay leaves,
and cook until the carrot and celery are soft. Add the
tomatoes and cook for a further 5 minutes. Remove and
discard the bay leaves.

**3** Sauté the meatballs in a little olive oil until golden
brown. Transfer them to the sauce and season to taste
with salt and pepper.

**4** Cook the macaroni in boiling salted water for about
5 minutes until just tender, then drain and refresh.

**5** Meanwhile, sauté the peppers quickly in the
remaining oil until they are tender but still firm. Mix
with the macaroni and season with salt and pepper.
Arrange on individual serving plates and top with a
little sauce. Garnish with the meatballs and some
chopped basil.

**Wine:** *Valpolicella Classico Antanel Villa Spinosa
1992 (Italy)*

# CAESAR SALAD *with* CHORIZO SAUSAGE

This is an old-time favourite served with a new twist. If preferred, you can substitute any poultry, fish or shellfish for the Chorizo sausage.

### SERVES 4

*4 slices white bread, crusts removed*
*2 Cos lettuces, cut into 5-cm (2-in) pieces*
*25 g (1 oz) Parmesan cheese, freshly grated*
*1 Chorizo sausage, cut into 6-mm (1/4-in) slices*

*For the dressing:*
*3 egg yolks*
*1 garlic clove, crushed*
*2 anchovy fillets*
*2 tablespoons finely chopped shallot*
*1 teaspoon English mustard*
*1 teaspoon Worcestershire sauce*
*2 tablespoons Balsamic vinegar*
*1/2 small red chilli, seeded and chopped*
*100 ml (31/2 fl oz) olive oil*
*salt and freshly ground black pepper*

**1** Cut the bread into 1-cm (1/2-in) squares and place on a baking tray. Toast in a preheated oven at 190°C, 375°F, Gas Mark 5 for 15-20 minutes, until crisp and golden, turning occasionally. Leave to cool. If wished, the croûtons can be made in advance and stored in an airtight container.

**2** Make the dressing. Put the egg yolks, garlic, anchovy fillets, shallot, mustard, Worcestershire sauce, balsamic vinegar and chilli in a liquidizer or blender. With the motor running, add the olive oil very slowly through the feed tube, until it forms a thick sauce. Season to taste with salt and pepper.

**3** Mix the lettuce and Parsmean cheese in a large bowl, add the dressing and toss well until all the leaves are just coated with the dressing.

**4** Transfer the salad to four deep soup plates, garnish with Chorizo sausage and garnish with the croûtons.

**Wine:** *Pouilly Fumé, Serge Dagenneau 1993 (Burgundy)*

# WILD MUSHROOMS *and* BABY ARTICHOKES IN PUMPKIN SEED OIL

Although pumpkin seed oil is relatively new, it is now available in many supermarkets and delicatessens. You can substitute walnut, grapeseed or, indeed, a good olive oil, if wished.

### SERVES 4

*4 baby artichokes*
*50 ml (2 fl oz) olive oil*
*115 g (4 oz) wild mushrooms (cepes, girolles, oyster, black trumpets)*
*4 tablespoons pumpkin seed oil*
*3 tablespoons balsamic vinegar*
*400 g (14 oz) haricot verts, trimmed, cooked and refreshed*
*1 large shallot, finely chopped*
*salt and freshly ground black pepper*

1 Remove the stalks and rough outside leaves from the artichokes and cut each one into six pieces. Heat two-thirds of the olive oil in a heavy non-stick pan and cook the artichokes slowly until softened. Remove and cool, and season with salt and pepper.

2 Clean the wild mushrooms carefully. Leave whole or cut them in half, depending on their size. Dip them into boiling salted water for approximately 20 seconds, remove and drain.

3 Heat the remaining olive oil and gently sauté the mushrooms until softened. Remove and season to taste with salt and pepper.

4 Mix the pumpkin seed oil with the balsamic vinegar and a little seasoning. Mix the haricots verts, mushrooms and shallot in one-third of the dressing and arrange in the centre of each serving plate. Gently toss the artichokes in half of the remaining dressing and arrange them around the mushrooms. Sprinkle with the remaining dressing and serve.

**Wine:** *Barbaresco Riserva 1990 (Italy)*

# ASPARAGUS WONTONS *with* ALMOND AIOLI

This very simple dish makes an unusual first course and is packed with delicate flavours.
You can also serve the Almond Aioli with fish soups.

### SERVES 4

100 g (3¹/2 oz) pearl barley
1 small onion, finely chopped
50 ml (2 fl oz) vegetable oil
2 garlic cloves, crushed
¹/2 leek, trimmed and chopped
1 carrot, diced
1 small fennel bulb, trimmed and diced
1 stick celery, diced
200 ml (7 fl oz) dry white wine
800 ml (1 pint 7 fl oz) water
2 star anise, crushed
¹/4 teaspoon black peppercorns
¹/2 bay leaf
¹/4 teaspoon coriander seeds
2 shallots, finely chopped
12 asparagus spears, peeled, blanched, cut in half and sliced thinly
115 g (4 oz) Ricotta cheese
12 wonton wrappers
1 tablespoon chopped fresh chives
salt and freshly ground black pepper
4 asparagus tips, to garnish
100 ml (3¹/2 fl oz) Almond Aioli (see opposite)

**1** Soak the pearl barley in cold water for 2 hours, changing the water twice. Drain, then season and simmer until cooked. Drain and refresh.

**2** Sweat the onions in a little of the oil until soft and translucent. Add one of the garlic cloves and cook for 1 minute. Stir in the leek, carrot, onion, fennel and celery, cover the pan and sweat for 2 minutes. Add the white wine, water, salt and pepper.

**3** Put the star anise in a piece of muslin with the peppercorns, bay leaf and coriander seeds and tie securely. Add to the vegetables and simmer for 20 minutes. Stir in the pearl barley and cook for 5 minutes.

**4** Sweat the shallots in the remaining oil until soft and translucent. Add the remaining garlic and cook gently for 1 minute. Remove from the heat and cool. Stir in the asparagus and ricotta cheese and season to taste.

**5** Lay out the wontons and place a teaspoon of the cheese mixture in the middle of each. Brush the edges with water and pull all four corners up to the top and press together firmly. Blanch in boiling salted water.

**6** Place two wontons in each dish and add the broth. Sprinkle with chives and serve with Almond Aioli.

**Wine:** *Muscat 1993 (Alsace)*

# FETA *and* ROCKET SALAD *with* BALSAMIC ONIONS

The onions are a sheer delight in this easily prepared dish. You can use the onions in other hot and cold dishes as they have a wonderful flavour and texture.

### SERVES 4

*20 button onions, peeled*
*4 tablespoons extra-virgin olive oil*
*100 ml (3½ fl oz) balsamic vinegar*
*100 g (3½ oz) puy lentils*
*1-2 tablespoons sherry vinegar, to taste*
*50 g (2 oz) home-dried tomatoes in olive oil (see page 55)*
*50 g (2 oz) rocket*
*25 g (1 oz) baby spinach, washed and trimmed*
*225 g (8 oz) feta cheese, cubed*
*small bunch of flat-leaf parsley, chopped*
*salt and freshly ground black pepper*

1 Pack the onions tightly into a small heavy-based saucepan. Add 2 tablespoons of the olive oil and fry over fierce heat for 5 minutes, or until brown. Turn the onions so that they colour evenly. Reduce the heat, cover the pan and cook for 5 minutes, or until tender.

2 Transfer the onions to a small bowl and pour the balsamic vinegar over them. Cover and leave in a cool place to marinate for at least 12 hours. They can be kept in the refrigerator, covered, for up to two weeks – and you can reuse the balsamic vinegar.

3 Wash the lentils and cook in plenty of salted water for about 25 minutes, until they are just tender and retain some 'bite'. Drain, refresh in cold water and dry on a clean tea towel.

4 Mix the sherry vinegar with the remaining oil to make a dressing and season to taste. Mix three-quarters of this dressing with the lentils and dried tomatoes. Spoon on to four serving plates.

5 Toss the rocket, spinach and drained button onions with half of the remaining dressing. Arrange on top of the lentils and scatter with feta cheese and parsley. Pour the remaining dressing over the cheese.

*Wine: Soave Classico DOC Villata 1993*

## ALMOND AIOLI

### MAKES: 300 ML (½ PINT)

*3 garlic cloves, peeled*
*½ teaspoon salt*
*50 g (2 oz) ground almonds*
*3 tablespoons white wine vinegar or lemon juice*
*2 egg yolks*
*250 ml (9 fl oz) olive oil*

1 Crush the garlic with the salt in a mortar. Mix in the ground almonds, vinegar or lemon juice and the egg yolks.

2 Using a wooden spoon or an electric hand mixer, incorporate the olive oil, adding it drop by drop until the mixture thickens to the consistency of mayonnaise.

# FESTIVE FISH

At Christmas, we tend to eat so much seasonal meat, poultry and game that fish makes a beautifully light and revitalizing alternative, especially after all the traditional rich food and sauces of Christmas Eve and Christmas Day. Order fresh fish from your fishmonger well in advance and pick it up on Christmas Eve. If you cannot obtain fresh fish, you can use frozen. Here are some simple but elegant dishes that you can serve to your family and friends.

# BRILL *with* TOMATOES *and* COURGETTES

With its light, refined blend of flavours, this dish is ideal for Boxing Day when you are still
recovering from the rich and heavy food of Christmas Day.

### SERVES 4

*4 x 150 g (5 oz) fillets of brill, skin and bones removed*
*2 plum tomatoes, skinned and sliced*
*2 small courgettes, blanched and sliced*
*3 tablespoons vegetable oil*
*115 g (4 oz) streaky bacon rashers, rind removed*
*3 tablespoons sherry vinegar*
*juice of 1/2 lime*
*4 handfuls mixed salad leaves (rocket, curly endive, baby spinach)*
*25 g (1oz) pine nuts, toasted*
*4 tablespoons balsamic vinegar*
*salt and freshly ground black pepper*

1 Season the fillets of brill with salt and pepper and place on an oiled baking tray. Arrange the sliced tomatoes and courgettes on top and season lightly. Brush with a little of the oil and cook in a preheated oven at 200°C, 400°F, Gas Mark 6 for 8-10 minutes.

2 Meanwhile, cook the bacon rashers under a preheated hot grill until crisp on both sides. Remove and cut into thin strips.

3 Mix the remaining oil with the sherry vinegar and lime juice. Season to taste and dress the salad leaves.

4 Place the cooked brill, tomatoes and courgettes in the centre of each serving plate. Arrange the salad leaves around the brill and sprinkle with warm toasted pine nuts, the crisp bacon strips and balsamic vinegar.

***Wine:*** *Chianti Classico 1990 (Italy)*

# HADDOCK *in* TEMPURA

Most of us enjoy haddock, but this is served in a feather-light tempura batter with a warm
potato salad instead of the traditional chips.

### SERVES 4

*2 eggs*
*120 ml (4 fl oz) iced water*
*generous pinch of bicarbonate of soda*
*100 g (3½ oz) plain flour*
*8 x 75 g (3 oz) pieces of haddock, skin and bones removed*
*vegetable oil for deep frying*
*salt and pepper*

***For the warm potato salad:***
*600 g (1¼ lb) new potatoes in their skins*
*½ teaspoon caraway seeds (optional)*
*1 small onion, finely chopped*
*5-cm (2-in) piece of cucumber, peeled and finely sliced*
*50 ml (2 fl oz) chicken stock*
*3 tablespoons white wine vinegar*
*50 ml (2 fl oz) vegetable oil*
*salt and freshly ground black pepper*

1 Make the potato salad. Scrub the potatoes but do not
peel them. Place in a saucepan and cover with cold
water. Add a little salt and the caraway seeds (optional)
and bring to the boil. Reduce the heat and simmer gently
for about 15 minutes, until tender. Drain well and cut the
potatoes into 5-mm (¼-in) thick slices.

2 Mix the potatoes with the onion, cucumber, chicken
stock, white wine vinegar, oil, salt and pepper. Be
very gentle so as not to break the potatoes. Put aside
and keep warm.

3 Make the tempura batter. Whisk the eggs and water
together until pale. Whisk in the bicarbonate of soda
and 60 g (2½ oz) of the flour. Take care not to over-
whisk the batter.

4 Season the haddock pieces and turn them in the
remaining flour. Dip them into the tempura batter
and then deep fry in vegetable oil at 190°C, 375°F, until
crisp and golden brown. Remove and dry on absorbent
kitchen paper.

5 Serve the haddock immediately accompanied by the
warm potato salad.

**Wine:** *Chardonnay 1992 (California)*

# PLAITED SOLE *with* KING PRAWNS

This delightful dish is easy to prepare. You can vary it by using any fish or vegetables of your choice.

### SERVES 4

4 x 75 g (3 oz) fillets of sole
2 tablespoons olive oil
50 g (2 oz) butter
2 garlic cloves, peeled
4 king prawns, shelled
pinch of saffron strands
200 ml (7 fl oz) double cream
1 teaspoon lemon juice
4 baby fennel, cooked in salted water
12 baby carrots, blanched
12 mangetout, blanched
25 g (1 oz) flaked almonds, toasted
sprigs of fresh dill, to garnish
salt and pepper

1 Cut each fillet of sole into three strips lengthwise and plait together. Heat the oil and half of the butter and add the garlic cloves. Cook for 1 minute and remove from the pan. Add the sole and king prawns and sauté until just cooked, about 4-5 minutes. Remove and keep warm.

2 Add the saffron, cream and lemon juice to the pan juices and simmer until the sauce thickens slightly. Season to taste with salt and pepper.

3 Heat the prepared vegetables in the remaining butter and season with salt and pepper.

4 Place a little sauce in the centre of each serving plate and arrange the sole, king prawns and vegetables on the plate. Serve garnished with toasted almonds and dill.

*Wine: Saint Véran, Michel Paquet 1994 (Burgundy)*

# HAKE *with* CREAMED FLAGEOLET BEANS

I always feel that flageolet beans are very underrated. They go well with almost any
fish or meat and are great for stewed dishes.

SERVES **4**

200 g (7 oz) dried flageolet beans
400 ml (14 fl oz) chicken stock or water
1 small onion, finely chopped
25 g (1 oz) butter
1 garlic clove, crushed
100 ml (3¹/₂ fl oz) double cream
4 plum tomatoes, skinned, seeded and diced
4 bay leaves
oil for deep frying
3 tablespoons vegetable oil
4 x 150 g (5 oz) hake fillets, bones removed
juice of ¹/₂ lemon
salt and freshly ground black pepper

**1** Soak the flageolet beans for 1 hour in cold water, changing the water twice. Drain and place the beans in a large saucepan with the chicken stock or water. Simmer gently for 1¹/₂ hours, until the beans are very soft. Top up with more water if necessary while the beans are cooking – they must be covered all the time. When cooked, drain the beans, reserving the cooking liquid.

**2** Sweat the onion in two-thirds of the butter until soft and translucent. Add the garlic and cook gently for 1 minute. Add the bean liquor and cream, increase the heat and reduce by half. Add the tomatoes and beans and season to taste.

**3** Deep fry the bay leaves in some oil until crisp. Remove from the pan and dry them on absorbent kitchen paper.

**4** Heat the vegetable oil in a non-stick frying pan and add the fish, skin-side down. Fry quickly until the skin is very crisp and the fish is nearly cooked. Turn the hake over and add the remaining butter and lemon juice. Fry gently until the fish is cooked – the flesh should be opaque and moist when the point of a knife is inserted.

**5** Arrange the creamed bean mixture on four serving plates, top with the fried hake and garnish with the deep fried bay leaves.

**Wine:** *Sauvignon Blanc 1994 (New Zealand)*

# BRILL FILLETS *with* CAPONATA

You do not have to use brill in this Mediterranean-style dish. Any white fish can be
substituted, including cod, halibut or haddock.

### SERVES 4

*vegetable oil for deep/shallow frying*
*8 sage leaves, cut into strips*
*200 g (7 oz) potatoes, peeled and cut into strips, 10 cm (4 in) long and 2 mm ($^1/_8$ in) wide*
*1 small onion, finely chopped*
*4 tablespoons olive oil*
*1 garlic clove, crushed*
*1 aubergine, diced*
*200 ml (7 fl oz) chicken or vegetable stock*
*250 g (9 oz) tomatoes, skinned, seeded and diced*
*4 x 150 g (5 oz) fillets of brill, skin and bones removed*
*1 teaspoon finely chopped fresh thyme*
*1 teaspoon lemon juice*
*100 ml (3$^1/_2$ fl oz) dry white wine*
*salt and freshly ground black pepper*

1 Heat the vegetable oil to 120°C, 250°F and fry the
sage leaves until crisp, Remove and drain on
absorbent kitchen paper. Increase the temperature to
180°C, 350°F and fry the potatoes until golden brown.
Dry on kitchen paper, mix with the sage and keep warm.

2 Sweat the onion in half of the olive oil until soft and
translucent. Add the garlic and cook for 1 minute.
Add the aubergine, season with salt and pepper and cook
for 3 minutes. Add half the stock and cook rapidly,
stirring occasionally, until the stock has evaporated. Add
the tomatoes, check the seasoning and remove from the
heat.

3 Season the brill with salt and pepper and half of the
chopped thyme. Heat the remaining olive oil in a non-
stick frying pan and fry the brill very quickly until cooked
and evenly brown. Remove and keep warm.

4 Pour the oil away and add the lemon juice, white
wine and the remaining stock to the pan. Reduce by
two-thirds over high heat, and season lightly with salt
and pepper.

5 Place a spoonful of the aubergine mixture on each
serving plate and top with the brill and potatoes.
Pour a little of the reduced wine and stock around the fish
and sprinkle with the remaining thyme.

*Wine: Sancerre 1994 (Loire)*

# GRILLED SALMON *and* SCALLOPS *with a* SPICY SAUCE

This dish is not as complicated as it looks but you must take care not to overcook it. The sauce is very versatile and also goes well with poultry and vegetable dishes.

### SERVES 4

*4 x 75 g (3 oz) fillets of salmon (with skin)*
*4 x 40 g (1¹/₂ oz) scallops*
*40 g (1¹/₂ oz) butter*
*1 tablespoon oil*
*1 onion, finely chopped*
*1 red pepper, seeded and diced*
*1 apple, peeled, cored and diced*
*¹/₂ teaspoon curry powder*
*pinch of saffron (optional)*
*400 ml (14 fl oz) chicken or vegetable stock*
*2 tablespoons double cream or crème fraîche*
*2 large courgettes*
*2 large carrots, peeled*
*2 large kohlrabi, peeled*
*1 tablespoon groundnut oil*
*salt and pepper*
*sprigs of fresh dill, to garnish*

**1** Scale the skin on the salmon fillets and then remove and set aside. Discard any brown flesh, cut the fillets in half and trim to the same depth as the scallops.

**2** Wrap two pieces of salmon around each scallop and overlap the thin ends of the salmon. Cut the reserved salmon skin into strips the same height as the salmon. Wrap the skin around the salmon and scallop rolls.

**3** Heat half the butter with the oil and cook the onion, stirring frequently, until it is soft and translucent. Add the red pepper and cook gently, covered, for 10 minutes. Stir in the apple, curry powder and saffron and cook for a further 5 minutes. Add the stock and bring to the boil. Cover the pan and simmer for 20 minutes.

**4** Purée the sauce in a blender and then pass it through a fine sieve into a clean saucepan, pressing down on the vegetables in the sieve to extract maximum liquid and flavour. Season with salt and pepper, stir in the cream or crème fraîche and set aside.

**5** Peel the green skin off the courgettes and then cut them into strips, 3 mm (¹/₈ in) wide and 10 cm (4 in) long. Cut the carrots and kohlrabi into strips in the same way. Blanch all the vegetables quickly in salted water until just tender and refresh in iced water.

**6** Season the salmon rolls with salt and pepper. Turn them in groundnut oil and cook under a preheated grill until the fish is translucent and moist.

**7** Melt the remaining butter and toss the courgettes, carrots and kohlrabi. Season to taste and arrange neatly on four serving plates. Place a salmon portion on each plate and pour the sauce around it. Garnish with dill.

**Wine:** *Hautes Côtes de Beaune Rollin 1994 (Burgundy)*

# TRADITIONAL MEAT AND POULTRY

One of the great pleasures of Christmas is the sheer variety of seasonal meat, poultry and game. Pheasant, partridge, duck, turkey, grouse and venison are all plentiful at this time of year. Here are some sophisticated recipes for festive dinner parties as well as more homely, robust dishes such as Game Pie and Guinness Braised Ham with Root Vegetables.

# PARTRIDGES *on* MARINATED CABBAGE

This is a wonderfully robust winter dish. Ideally, the cabbage should be cooked the day
before as it tastes better when reheated.

### SERVES 4

*75 g (3 oz) smoked streaky bacon rashers*
*115 g (4 oz) thinly sliced onion*
*50 ml (2 fl oz) groundnut oil*
*450 g (1 lb) sauerkraut, washed well in cold water and drained*
*100 ml (3½ fl oz) dry white wine*
*200 ml (7 fl oz) chicken stock*
*½ bay leaf*
*2 juniper berries*
*2 large carrots*
*4 oven-ready partridges*
*200 g (7 oz) garlic sausages*
*salt and freshly ground black pepper*

**1** Put the bacon in a pan of cold water and bring to the boil. Simmer for 10 minutes. Drain and refresh in cold water.

**2** Sweat the onion in a little of the oil in a flameproof casserole until soft and translucent. Add the washed and drained sauerkraut, white wine, chicken stock, bay leaf, juniper berries, bacon and carrots. Bring to the boil, cover with a lid and cook in a preheated oven at 200°C, 400°F, Gas Mark 6 for 1 hour, stirring frequently.

**3** Season the partridges inside and out with salt and pepper. Heat the remaining oil in a roasting pan and turn the partridges in it. Lay them on one side and roast in the preheated oven for 5 minutes. Turn them over on to the other side and roast for 5 minutes. Turn them over on to their backs and roast for a further 5 minutes. Remove from the oven and cool slightly.

**4** Cut each partridge in half and remove the bones. Place them in the casserole with the garlic sausage, and return to the oven for another 30 minutes.

**5** Remove from the oven and season the sauerkraut to taste. Cut the rind off the bacon and cut into slices. Remove the skin from the garlic sausage and cut into slices. Slice the carrots.

**6** Arrange the partridges with the sauerkraut, bacon and garlic sausage on each serving plate and garnish with the carrots.

*Wine: Gewurztraminer 1993 (Alsace)*

# ROAST PHEASANT *with* LENTIL RAGOUT

If possible, use hen pheasants for this recipe and hang them for at least four days.
Puy lentils are far superior to the normal ones and are easily available from most supermarkets.
To get the best flavour from the lentils, they should be heated twice.

### SERVES 4

2 hen pheasants, dressed with thin rashers of bacon
100 ml (3¹/₂ fl oz) vegetable oil
40 g (1¹/₂ oz) unsalted butter
1 onion, finely chopped
2 garlic cloves, crushed
100 g (3¹/₂ oz) smoked bacon, cut into 5-mm (¹/₄-in) strips
¹/₂ tablespoon tomato purée
200 g (7 oz) puy lentils
600 ml (1 pint) chicken stock
20 button onions, peeled
salt and freshly ground black pepper

1 Remove the wishbone from each pheasant. Season them inside and out with salt and pepper and place each on its side in a roasting pan with a little of the oil. Roast in a preheated oven at 200 °C, 400°F, Gas Mark 6 for 10 minutes. Turn them on to the other side and roast for a further 10 minutes. Then turn them on to their backs, baste with the pan fat and juices and continue roasting for 10 more minutes. Remove the pheasants and bacon from the pan and keep warm.

2 Meanwhile, melt half of the butter in a heavy-based pan with a little of the oil and cook the chopped onion until soft and translucent. Add the garlic and cook for 1 minute. Add the bacon strips and continue cooking until golden and crisp.

3 Add the tomato purée and cook until lightly caramelized, stirring continuously. Stir in the lentils and the stock, bring to the boil and then reduce the heat and simmer until the lentils are cooked, stirring occasionally.

4 Heat the remaining oil in a heavy-based pan and pack in the button onions to just fill the bottom of the pan in a single layer. Fry over high heat until they are evenly coloured on all sides. Season with salt and pepper, cover the pan and cook over gentle heat until tender.

5 Add the onions to the lentil mixture and adjust the seasoning. Pour the juices from the pheasants into the mixture, and arrange on four serving plates.

6 Carve the breasts and legs off the pheasants and place on top of the lentils and onions. Garnish with the reserved crisp roasted bacon rashers.

**Wine:** *Santenay Beaurepaire 1989 (Burgundy)*

# BABY TURKEY BREAST *with* CHESTNUT STUFFING

Not having to cook the legs means that the breast is nice and moist. Also you will not have to eat endless turkey sandwiches!

SERVES 6

50 g (2 oz) onions, finely chopped
50 ml (2 fl oz) groundnut oil
200 g (7 oz) sausagemeat
200 g (7 oz) chestnut purée
500 ml (18 fl oz) turkey or chicken stock
800 g (1lb 12 oz) turkey breast, boned and skinned
1 small bunch sage leaves
4 slices Parma ham
400 g (14 oz) vegetables for roasting, e.g. carrots, garlic, leeks, parsnips, red onion, corn cobs
200 g (7 oz) turkey bones, chopped (wings, neck etc.)
115 g (4 oz) chopped vegetables, e.g. onion, celery, carrot, green part of leek
2 cloves garlic
1 tablespoon tomato purée
200 ml (7 fl oz) dry white wine
1/2 bay leaf and 2 sprigs thyme
salt and pepper

1 Sweat the onions in a little of the oil until soft and translucent. Add the sausagemeat and cook, stirring occasionally, until well done. Stir in the chestnut purée and, if necessary, a little of the stock. Season and continue cooking for a few minutes.

2 Remove the fillet from the turkey breast and place it between 2 sheets of plastic or greaseproof paper. Flatten it out with a meat bat. Make an incision lengthways down the middle of the breast, cutting two-thirds into the flesh. Make a sideways incision on both sides of the breast so that it opens out like an envelope.

3 Fill the breast with the stuffing and place the fillet over the top. Fold the sides over into the middle to make a neat bundle. Spread some sage leaves on top and wrap the Parma ham around. Tie with string.

4 Heat a little oil in a roasting pan and add the breast. Turn it over in the oil and surround with vegetables of your choice. Place in a preheated oven at 200°C, 400°F, Gas Mark 6 for 40 minutes, basting the turkey regularly.

5 Meanwhile, roast the turkey bones in another roasting pan until browned, adding the chopped vegetables and garlic for a further 5 minutes. Remove from the oven and add the tomato purée and white wine. Place over high heat and boil until the gravy mixture reduces and the tomato purée caramelizes. Add the turkey or chicken stock, herbs and seasoning, and simmer for 20 minutes, skimming frequently. Pass through a fine sieve, return to the pan and cook steadily until reduced by half. Season to taste.

6 Remove the turkey breast and vegetables and keep warm. Pour away the fat in the pan and add the prepared turkey gravy. Stir well, scraping any sediment off the bottom of the pan into the gravy. Slice the turkey breast and serve with the roast vegetables and gravy.

**Wine:** *De Redcliffe, Marlborough Sauvignon 1993 (New Zealand)*

# PORK OLIVES *with* LEMON COUS-COUS STUFFING

Take care not to overcook the pork or it will lose its juices and flavour. The cous-cous is sensational –
you can eat it on its own or serve it with poultry, lamb and even fish.

### SERVES 4

*8 x 50 g (2 oz) pork fillets*
*50 ml (2 fl oz) vegetable oil*
*50 g (2 oz) unsalted butter*
*1 onion, finely chopped*
*50 g (2 oz) chicken livers, cleaned and roughly chopped*
*250 ml (8 fl oz) white wine*
*200 ml (7 fl oz) chicken stock*
*200 g (7 oz) cous-cous*
*finely grated zest of 1 lemon*
*25 g (1 oz) raisins, soaked and squeezed*
*1 teaspoon fresh thyme*
*8 thin rashers streaky bacon*
*salt and pepper*

**1** Place the pork fillets between two sheets of greaseproof paper and hit them with a mallet or rolling pin to flatten them. They should be about 3 mm (1/8 in) thick and 12.5 cm (5 in) square.

**2** Heat a little of the oil and butter in a pan and cook the onion gently until soft and translucent. Add the chicken livers, and season with salt and pepper. Add half of the wine and half of the chicken stock and stir in the cous-cous. Turn up the heat and continue stirring until the mixture boils. Reduce the heat and simmer, covered, for 10-15 minutes until the cous-cous is tender and all the liquid has been absorbed. Add the grated lemon zest, raisins and thyme, and adjust the seasoning.

**3** Divide the cous-cous stuffing between the pork fillets. Spread it out evenly over each fillet and then roll up tightly. Wrap a bacon rasher around each pork roll and secure with a wooden cocktail stick.

**4** Heat the remaining oil and some of the butter and brown the pork olives on all sides. Transfer to a baking pan, cover and cook in a preheated oven at 200°C, 400°F, Gas Mark 6 for about 10 minutes, turning them once or twice. Remove the pork olives from the pan and keep warm.

**5** Pour away the fat from the pan, then add the remaining wine and reduce over high heat by two-thirds. Add the rest of the stock and cook rapidly until reduced by half. Remove from the heat and cool slightly. Whisk in the remaining butter, season to taste and pass through a fine sieve.

**6** Remove the cocktail sticks from the pork olives and cut into slices. Arrange on four serving plates and pour the sauce around them.

**Wine:** *Fleurie 1995 (Beaujolais)*

# CHICKEN *with* CINNAMON STUFFING

The beauty of this dish is the cinnamon stuffing which gives it a real bite.

### SERVES 4

*40 g (1¹/2 oz) dried apricots, soaked overnight*
*50 g (2 oz) fresh white breadcrumbs*
*finely grated zest of ¹/2 lemon*
*¹/2 apple, peeled, cored and chopped*
*¹/2 teaspoon ground cinnamon*
*40 g (1¹/2 oz) unsalted butter, melted*
*1 tablespoon chopped walnuts*
*1 crumbled goat's cheese, e.g. Crottin*
*2 x 1 kg (2¹/4 lb) maize-fed chickens*
*50 ml (2 fl oz) vegetable oil*
*50 ml (2 fl oz) dry white wine*
*400 ml (14 fl oz) Chicken Gravy (see page 51)*
*salt and freshly ground black pepper*

**1** Cut the soaked apricots into small cubes and mix with the breadcrumbs, lemon zest, apple, cinnamon, two-thirds of the melted butter, the walnuts and goat's cheese.

**2** Remove the wishbone from the chickens and season inside and out. Fill the chickens with the stuffing from the front, pull over the skin and sew it up.

**3** Heat the remaining butter and oil in a roasting pan. Place the chickens in the pan on their sides and roast in a preheated oven at 200°C, 400°F, Gas Mark 6. After 20 minutes, turn the chickens over on to the other side.

After another 20 minutes, turn them on to their backs and roast for 30 minutes, basting frequently. Remove from the pan and keep warm.

**4** Pour away the fat, add the white wine to the pan and reduce by half over high heat. Add the chicken gravy and reduce a little more. Season to taste and pass through a fine sieve.

**5** Cut the chickens at the joints into neat pieces and serve with the stuffing and sauce.

***Wine:*** *Semillon Sauvignon Blanc 1994 (Australia)*

# GUINNESS BRAISED HAM *with* ROOT VEGETABLES

I always enjoy a traditional dish like this. The sweetness of the honey and the bitterness of the
Guinness perfectly complement the ham and add flavour to the root vegetables.

SERVES 8

2 kg (4 lb) gammon joint
5 tablespoons brown sugar
200 ml (7 fl oz) Guinness
100 g (3¹/₂ oz) carrot
100 g (3¹/₂ oz) swede
100 g (3¹/₂ oz) turnip
100 g (3¹/₂ oz) parsnip

1 Soak the gammon in cold water for 4 hours, changing the water frequently. Drain and place the gammon in

## RED WINE *and* ONION MARMALADE

This is very versatile and can be served with
virtually any fish, meat or poultry.

100 ml (3¹/₂ fl oz) vegetable oil
500 g (1 lb 2 oz) red onions, thinly sliced
50 ml (2 fl oz) red wine vinegar
200 ml (7 fl oz) red wine
1 teaspoon redcurrant jelly

1 Heat the oil in a thick-based pan and add the onions. Cover with a lid and cook very slowly until the onions are soft and translucent.

2 Add the red wine vinegar, increase the heat and reduce. Add the red wine and redcurrant jelly and reduce again until the mixture thickens.

a large saucepan. Cover with fresh water and simmer for 2 hours 20 minutes, until tender. Remove the gammon from the pan, cool and cut off all but 5 mm (¹/₄ in) of the thick fat on the outside of the joint.

2 Mix the sugar and Guinness together and heat gently in a saucepan until the sugar is dissolved and the liquid is reduced by one-third. Place the gammon in a roasting pan, brush with some of the Guinness mixture and bake in a preheated oven at 180°C, 350°F, Gas Mark 4 for 45 minutes, basting frequently with the Guinness mixture.

3 Meanwhile, cut all the vegetables into strips, 5 cm (2 in) long by 1 cm (¹/₂ in) wide. After the gammon has been cooking for 20 minutes, add the carrots. Add the remaining vegetables 10 minutes later.

4 When the vegetables are tender, remove them from the pan and keep warm. Increase the oven temperature to 220°C, 425°F, Gas Mark 7. Brush the gammon with the remaining Guinness mixture, return to the oven and glaze until golden brown.

**Wine:** *Cabernet Sauvignon 1993 (Chile)*

# GAME PIE

### SERVES 4

*1 oven-ready grouse or pheasant and 1 oven-ready partridge, cut in half*
*200 g (7 oz) loin or haunch of venison, cut in half*
*25 g (1 oz) plain flour*
*50 ml (2 fl oz) oil*
*75 g (3 oz) unsalted butter*
*50 g (2 oz)* mirepoix *(finely chopped leek, celery, onion and carrot)*
*1 garlic clove, crushed*
*25 g (1 oz) tomato purée*
*200 ml (7 fl oz) red wine*
*300 ml (1/2 pint) chicken stock*
*1/2 bay leaf and 1 sprig of thyme*
*24 peppercorns, crushed, plus salt and freshly ground black pepper*
*25 g (1 oz) skinned and seeded plum tomato, chopped*
*15 g (1/2 oz) sugar*
*100 ml (31/2 fl oz) dry white wine*
*200 g (7 oz) chestnuts, shelled*
*50 g (2 oz) button mushrooms*
*50 g (2 oz) dried apricots, soaked for 1 hour*
*50 g (2 oz) button onions, blanched*
*50 g (2 oz) streaky bacon, cut in lardons and blanched*
*150 g (5 oz) puff pastry*
*1 egg yolk, beaten*

**1** Season all the meats and dust with flour. Heat half of the oil and 25 g (1 oz) of the butter and fry until golden brown. Remove and discard any fat.

**2** Add the remaining oil and 15 g (1/2 oz) of the butter, then fry the *mirepoix* for 5 minutes, until lightly coloured. Add the garlic and tomato purée and cook for 2-3 minutes, stirring constantly. Add the red wine and reduce, then add the chicken stock, herbs, peppercorns and tomato.

**3** Add the meats, cover with a lid and braise in a preheated oven at 180°C, 350°F, Gas Mark 4 for 30 minutes, stirring occasionally. Remove the meats and sieve the sauce. Season to taste and stir in 15 g (1/2 oz) of the butter.

**4** Remove the bones from the game birds and divide the breasts and legs. Cut the venison into smaller pieces.

**5** Heat a little of the butter with the sugar and lightly caramelize. Add the white wine and reduce, then add the chestnuts and reduce until glazed.

**6** Sauté the mushrooms in the remaining butter, and add to the sauce with the apricots, chestnuts, button onions and bacon. Season to taste with salt and pepper. Place all the meat in a large pie dish and then pour the sauce over the top.

**7** Roll out the puff pastry and cover the pie. Garnish with the trimmings and criss-cross the surface with a knife. Rest for 20 minutes in a cool place, brush with egg yolk and bake in a preheated oven at 200°C, 400°F, Gas Mark 6 for 25 minutes.

**Wine:** *Riddoch Cabernet/Shiraz 1994 (Australia)*

# CALF'S LIVER *with* SHALLOTS

The less you do to calf's liver, the better it is. Always season it when it comes out of the pan.

### SERVES 4

*50 ml (2 fl oz) vegetable oil*
*50 g (2 oz) unsalted butter*
*200 g (7 oz) finely chopped shallots*
*1/2 garlic clove, crushed*
*50 ml (2 fl oz) white wine vinegar*
*200 ml (7 fl oz) dry white wine*
*15 g (1/2 oz) clear honey*
*2 teaspoons chopped mixed herbs (marjoram, rosemary, thyme)*
*600 g (1 1/4 lb) calf's liver*
*400 g (14 oz) Olive Oil Potato Purée (see page 55)*
*salt and freshly ground black pepper*

**1** Heat a little of the oil and butter in a heavy-based pan, and add the shallots. Cover with a lid and sweat the shallots until they are softened and translucent.

**2** Add the garlic and cook for 1 minute, then add the white wine vinegar and reduce over high heat. Add the white wine and reduce again. Stir in the honey and herbs, season to taste and keep warm.

**3** Peel the skin off the liver and cut into 8 thin slices. Heat the remaining butter and oil in a frying pan and quickly fry the liver on both sides so that it remains pink inside. Remove from the pan and season with salt and pepper.

**4** Arrange the potato purée on four serving plates, top with the liver and pour the sauce over the top.

**Wine:** *Amontillado Sherry*

---

*CHRISTMAS DRINKS*

## SLOE GIN

Harvest the sloes and make this warming festive drink in the autumn.

### MAKES 900 ML (1 1/2 PINTS)

*450 g (1 lb) sloes*
*900 ml (1 1/2 pints) gin*
*300 g (10 oz) sugar*
*4 blanched almonds (optional)*

**1** Prick the sloes all over with a needle and put them in a large jar or bottle with the gin and sugar. Bruise the almonds and add to the jar. Seal or cork the jar.

**2** Leave for 2-3 months, shaking occasionally to dissolve the sugar. The gin will turn pink.

**3** Strain through muslin and bottle. The flavour improves with keeping so lay it down for a year if you have the will power!

# BRAISED OXTAIL *on* CELERIAC PURÉE

It is a good idea to cook the oxtail and make the sauce the day before you plan to serve it.
Ask your butcher to bone the oxtail for you.

### SERVES 6

*2 boned oxtails*
*2 bay leaves*
*2 sage leaves*
*2 tablespoons vegetable oil*
*50 g (2 oz) chopped carrot*
*100 g (3½ oz) chopped onion*
*200 ml (7 fl oz) red wine*
*100 ml (3½ fl oz) Madeira*
*500 ml (18 fl oz) chicken stock*
*500 g (1 lb 2 oz) celeriac, peeled and cubed*
*150 ml (¼ pint) milk*
*50 g (2 oz) chilled unsalted butter*
*2 tablespoons chopped fresh parsley*
*salt and freshly ground black pepper*

**1** Season the oxtails with salt and pepper. Place the herbs on one oxtail and then place the other one on top with the wide ends over the thin ends. Fold over both end pieces, roll into a round shape and secure with kitchen thread.

**2** Heat the oil in a saucepan and fry the oxtail until well coloured on all sides. Throw away the oil and add the vegetables, wine, Madeira and chicken stock to the saucepan to cover the meat. Cover with a lid and cook in a preheated oven at 200°C, 400°F, Gas Mark 6 for 3½ hours, until the meat is really tender.

**3** Remove the meat, discard the thread and wrap tightly in cling film. Cool, then chill. Reduce the liquid by two-thirds and pass through a fine sieve.

**4** Cook the celeriac in the milk with a little salt and pepper until very soft. Pour away two-thirds of the milk, then purée the remaining milk and celeriac and stir in a little of the butter. Season to taste and keep warm.

**5** Cut the oxtail, still in the cling film, into 6-cm (2½-in) wide slices and wrap each slice in fresh cling film. Reheat in water or steam.

**6** Meanwhile, reheat the sauce and whisk in the remaining butter. Season to taste. Put some celeriac purée on each serving plate. Remove the cling film from the oxtail and arrange on top of the celeriac. Pour the sauce over the top and sprinkle with chopped parsley.

**Wine:** *Marqués de Riscal Reserva, Rioja 1990 (Spain)*

# SEASONAL SAUCES

## CHICKEN GRAVY

The colour of the gravy depends on the browning of
the bones and tomato purée.

**MAKES 700 ML (1 PINT 4 FL OZ) GRAVY**

*400 g (14 oz) chicken carcasses and bones*
*3 tablespoons vegetable oil*
*2 onions, chopped*
*2 carrots, chopped*
*1 leek, trimmed and chopped*
*1 celery stalk, chopped*
*2 tomatoes, chopped*
*75 g (3 oz) tomato purée*
*2 peeled garlic cloves*
*1 small bay leaf*
*1 sprig of thyme*
*250 ml (9 fl oz) dry white wine*
*2.5 litres (4 pints) chicken stock*
*salt and pepper*

**1** Chop the chicken carcasses and bones into small
pieces. Heat the oil in a roasting pan on top of the
stove and add the bones. Roast for 10 minutes in a
preheated oven at 220°C, 425°F, Gas Mark 7.

**2** Add all the chopped vegetables and continue
roasting for 10 minutes, or until the bones are
browned. Add the tomatoes, tomato purée, garlic cloves
and herbs. Stir well and roast for 10 more minutes.

**3** Pour the mixture into a large saucepan, scraping in
any pan residues. Add the wine to the roasting pan
and bring to the boil on top of the stove, stirring well.
Pour into the saucepan and then bring to the boil. Add
the stock and bring back to the boil, then simmer
gently until reduced by half, skimming occasionally.
Strain through muslin or a fine sieve.

## SPICY VEGETABLE SAUCE

This sweet and spicy sauce is an excellent
accompaniment to fish, poultry, pasta and
vegetable dishes.

**MAKES: 400 ML (14 FL OZ)**

*25 g (1 oz) unsalted butter*
*1½ tablespoons vegetable oil*
*1 onion, finely chopped*
*1 red pepper, cored, seeded and chopped*
*1 apple, peeled, cored and sliced*
*½ teaspoon curry powder*
*pinch of saffron (optional)*
*350 ml (12 fl oz) chicken stock*
*3 tablespoons double cream or*
*crème fraîche*
*salt and freshly ground black pepper*

**1** Heat the butter and oil in a saucepan and cook the
onion over low heat until softened and translucent,
stirring often. Stir in the red pepper, cover the pan and
cook gently for 10 minutes.

**2** Add the apple, curry powder and saffron (if
using) and stir well. Cook, covered, for a further
5 minutes. Add 300 ml (½ pint) of the chicken stock
and bring to the boil. Reduce the heat, cover the pan
and simmer gently for 20 minutes.

**3** Purée the sauce in a blender or food processor,
then pass through a fine sieve into a clean
saucepan, pressing down to extract maximum flavour
and liquid. Stir in the remaining stock and season
with salt and pepper. Reheat and stir in the cream
before serving.

# SEASONAL VEGETABLES

Vegetables are often overlooked at Christmas and play second fiddle to the traditional meat and poultry dishes. However, these recipes elevate humble vegetables to a more sublime level.

## BRAISED RED CABBAGE *with* PRUNES

To save time at Christmas, you can prepare this delicious red cabbage dish weeks in advance and store it in airtight jars in the refrigerator. You can ring the changes by using sugar-glazed chestnuts instead of prunes.

### SERVES 6

*1 kg (2¹/4 lb) red cabbage*
*200 ml (7 fl oz) red wine*
*100 g (3¹/2 oz) finely sliced onions*
*60 g (2¹/2 oz) goose fat or unsalted butter*
*40 g (1¹/2 oz) sugar*
*400 ml (14 fl oz) chicken stock*
*60 g (2¹/2 oz) prunes, soaked in Armagnac*
*2 cloves*
*¹/2 teaspoon black peppercorns*
*salt and freshly ground black pepper*

**1** Remove the outside leaves and stalk from the red cabbage, then slice it very thinly. Marinate for 10 minutes in the red wine.

**2** Sweat the onions in the goose fat or butter until softened and translucent. Add the sugar and cook gently for 1 minute until caramelized.

**3** Add the red cabbage and the wine in which it was marinated, and season with salt and pepper. Increase the heat and reduce the liquid, stirring frequently. Add the chicken stock and prunes.

**4** Wrap the cloves and peppercorns in a small piece of muslin and add to the cabbage. Cover with a lid and braise in a preheated oven at 180°C, 350°F, Gas Mark 4 for 2 hours, stirring occasionally.

**5** Remove from the oven, discard the muslin bag and season to taste with salt and pepper. The red cabbage can be eaten straight away or reheated – its flavour improves on reheating. Alternatively, pack into sterilized glass jars with screwtop lids and store in the refrigerator until required.

# BAKED CHICORY

Chicory is a much underrated vegetable which is more often found in salads, yet it tastes delicious cooked.

### SERVES 4

*4 heads chicory (Belgian endives)*
*2 tablespoons vegetable oil*
*25 g (1 oz) unsalted butter*
*25 g (1 oz) toasted almonds*
*salt and freshly ground black pepper*

1 Remove the damaged outside leaves from the chicory and trim the root ends. Place them in a thick-based pan with the oil and butter. Season with salt and pepper.

2 Bake in a preheated oven at 180°C, 350°F, Gas Mark 4 for 20 minutes. Remove the chicory and dry on kitchen paper. Serve sprinkled with toasted almonds.

# ROASTED VEGETABLES

You can roast almost any vegetables, either singly or several together. It is a good idea to mix colours, textures and flavours, using traditional root vegetables and more brightly coloured Mediterranean ones. The roasting times given below are a guideline and you should check them for tenderness – they should not be overcooked nor too hard. Choose a selection from those listed below and add them to the pan in sequence according to the suggested cooking time.

| Vegetable | Preparation | Cooking time | Vegetable | Preparation | Cooking time |
|---|---|---|---|---|---|
| Asparagus | Peel the stalks | 20 minutes | Carrots | Peel and leave whole | 45 minutes |
| Courgettes | Leave whole | 25 minutes | Celeriac | Peel and cut in cubes | 45 minutes |
| Broccoli | Separate into florets | 30 minutes | Onions | Peel and cut in half | 45 minutes |
| Leeks | Trim, wash, blanch | 30 minutes | Parsnips | Peel and quarter | 45 minutes |
| Cauliflower | Separate into florets | 40 minutes | Corn cobs | Leave whole | 50 minutes |
| Sweet potatoes | Peel and cut in half | 40 minutes | Potatoes | Peel and blanch | 50 minutes |

1 Heat a roasting pan over moderate heat and pour in sufficient vegetable oil or groundnut oil to make a film on the bottom.

2 Add the vegetables and turn to coat them in the oil. Season with salt and freshly ground black pepper and cook in a preheated oven at 200°C, 400°F, Gas Mark 6

for the suggested time. If wished, add a few sprigs of thyme or rosemary to the pan halfway through cooking.

3 Dot with a little unsalted butter 5 minutes before the end of the cooking time. When cooked, remove the vegetables from the pan and drain on absorbent kitchen paper, discarding the herbs.

# DELICIOUS DESSERTS

What better way is there to end a delicious meal in convivial company than with a stunning dessert? Many of the dishes featured incorporate traditional Christmas ingredients such as chestnuts, mincemeat and dried and candied fruits, albeit presented in an unusual and adventurous way. Try the sensational Christmas Pudding Ice Cream or Diana's Mincemeat Soufflé and give your old favourites a new twist.

# BLUEBERRY CHEESECAKE

For this recipe, you could use frozen wild blueberries but after defrosting you must drain them very well. If you cannot get ricotta cheese, use quark which is widely available in supermarkets.

### SERVES 8-10

*200 g (7 oz) shortbread biscuits, crumbled*
*300 g (10 oz) caster sugar*
*40 g (1¹/₂ oz) unsalted butter, melted*
*1 teaspoon ground cinnamon*
*225 g (8 oz) cream cheese*
*2 large eggs*
*1 egg yolk*
*225 g (8 oz) mascarpone cheese*
*225 g (8 oz) ricotta cheese, sieved*
*3 tablespoons ground almonds, toasted*
*1 tablespoon grated lemon zest*
*¹/₂ teaspoon vanilla extract*
*¹/₂ teaspoon almond extract*
*175 g (6 oz) fresh blueberries*
*icing sugar for dusting*

*For the strawberry coulis:*
*200 g (7 oz) strawberries, hulled and halved*
*50 g (2 oz) icing sugar*
*1 teaspoon lemon juice*

**1** Preheat the oven to 170°C, 325°F, Gas Mark 3. Combine the shortbread crumbs and 100 g (3¹/₂ oz) of the sugar with the melted butter and cinnamon. Mix until well blended. Press into the bottom and up the sides of a 20-cm (8-in) springform cake tin, and bake in the oven for 8 minutes. Remove from the oven and set aside.

**2** Beat the cream cheese with the remaining sugar. Gradually add the eggs and egg yolk. Beat in the mascarpone and then stir in the ricotta, ground almonds, grated lemon zest, and vanilla and almond extracts.

**3** Pour half of the cheese mixture into the prepared biscuit crust case and cover with half of the blueberries. Pour in the remaining cheese mixture and scatter the remaining blueberries over the top. Bake in the preheated oven for 40-50 minutes or until the filling is set. Turn off the oven and leave the cheesecake to cool in the oven for about 1 hour.

**4** When completely cool, transfer the cheesecake to the refrigerator and leave overnight or for at least 5 hours before cutting and serving.

**5** Make the strawberry coulis. Place the strawberries, icing sugar and lemon juice in a blender. Liquidize and then pass through a fine sieve.

**6** Serve the cheesecake, dusted lightly with icing sugar, with the strawberry coulis.

**Wine:** *Quail's Gate, Riesling Icewine 1993 (Canada)*

# BURNT ICE CREAM *with* GINGER

As with so many ice creams you can easily experiment with different flavours to vary the result.
Why not try substituting orange zest instead of lemon zest and a liqueur of your choice?

### SERVES 6

*800 ml (1 pint 7 fl oz) double cream*
*grated zest of 1 lemon*
*¼ cinnamon stick*
*6 egg yolks*
*300 g (10 oz) sugar*
*25 g (1 oz) candied stem ginger*

1 Heat the cream with the lemon zest and cinnamon stick almost to boiling point. Whisk the egg yolks with one-quarter of the sugar and then add the cream mixture, stirring all the time.

2 Return to the saucepan and bring to simmering point over low heat, stirring all the time until it coats the back of the spoon. Pass the custard through a fine sieve, add the candied stem ginger and cool.

3 Put the remaining sugar in a thick-based saucepan with a little water. Simmer gently, stirring until the sugar is completely dissolved, then continue simmering until the sugar caramelizes and turns a rich amber colour. Pour into a lightly buttered dish so that it forms a thin sheet. Leave to cool.

4 When the caramel sets, break up into small pieces and stir into the cream mixture. Pour into an ice cream machine, or into freezer trays and freeze. If you don't have an ice cream maker, remove the trays several times and stir well to break up the ice crystals.

*Wine: Rhine Beerenauslese 1990 (Germany)*

# PEARS FILLED *with* CHOCOLATE *and* AMARETTO SABAYON

Pears and chocolate complement each other well, and the Amaretto Sabayon adds
the finishing touches to a delicious dessert.

**SERVES 4**

*4 ripe but firm pears*
*175 g (6 oz) good-quality plain chocolate*
*200 g (7 oz) puff pastry*
*1 egg, beaten*

**For the Amaretto Sabayon:**
*5 egg yolks*
*75 g (3 oz) sugar*
*100 ml (3 1/2 fl oz) Amaretto*

**For the stock syrup:**
*1 litre (1 2/3 pints) water*
*500 g (1 lb 2 oz) sugar*
*1 cinnamon stick*

**1** Make the stock syrup. Heat the water and sugar in a saucepan over low heat and stir continuously until the sugar dissolves. Add the cinnamon stick and simmer gently to infuse the syrup with the cinnamon flavour and to thicken slightly.

**2** Peel the pears and remove the cores high inside each pear, using a parisienne scoop. Leave the stalks intact. Poach the pears for 2 minutes in the syrup, then remove and refresh.

**3** Melt the chocolate in the top of a double boiler or in a basin placed over a pan of simmering water. Place the pears, hollowed-out end down, in the melted chocolate. Remove and place in the refrigerator until set.

**4** Roll out the puff pastry thinly and wrap the pears in it. Brush the edges with beaten egg and press together well to seal them. Brush the pastry-covered pears all over with beaten egg and rest for 20 minutes in a cool place. Bake in a preheated oven at 190°C, 375°F, Gas Mark 5 for 20 minutes until golden brown.

**5** Make the Amaretto Sabayon. In a bowl over a pan of boiling water, whisk together the egg yolks, sugar and Amaretto until light and frothy.

**6** Place a pear in the centre of each serving dish and pour the Amaretto Sabayon around it.

**Wine:** *Essencia, Orange Muscat (California)*

# CHRISTMAS STOLLEN

Like Christmas pudding, this Stollen gets even better with age. You can serve tea or coffee with it.

### MAKES 1 STOLLEN

100 ml (3¹/2 fl oz) milk
1 vanilla pod, split open
15 g (¹/2 oz) fresh yeast
250 g (8¹/2 oz) strong plain flour
3 tablespoons caster sugar
pinch of salt
2 egg yolks
100 g (3¹/2 oz) unsalted butter, diced
100 g (3¹/2 oz) raisins
50 g (2 oz) mixed candied peel, chopped
finely grated zest and juice of 1 unwaxed lemon
1 tablespoon dark rum
40 g (1¹/2 oz) whole blanched almonds, toasted
50 g (2 oz) marzipan (optional)

*To finish:*
*melted unsalted butter and sifted icing sugar*

**1** Warm the milk with the vanilla pod. Cover and set aside to infuse for 20 minutes. Discard the vanilla pod and reheat the milk until it is lukewarm. Pour into a small bowl, add the yeast and mash with a spoon until creamy. Leave in a warm place for 10 minutes.

**2** Sift the flour, sugar and salt into a bowl. Pour in the yeast mixture, add the egg yolks and mix to form a soft dough. Knead for 5 minutes until smooth. Place the dough in a bowl, scatter the butter over it and cover with a damp cloth. Leave in a warm place for 2-2¹/2 hours, until doubled in bulk.

**3** Combine the raisins, candied peel, lemon zest and juice, and rum. Leave to macerate for 2 hours, then drain.

**4** Knead the risen dough gently, mixing in the butter. Add the drained fruit mixture and almonds and knead until the fruit and nuts are evenly distributed. Place in a bowl, cover and refrigerate for at least 4 hours.

**5** Turn out on to a cool floured surface and roll out to an oblong, 17.5 cm (7 in) by 12.5 cm (5 in), with one end thicker than the other and a dip in the centre. Shape the marzipan into a 'log', 10 cm (4 in) long, and place on the dough. Fold the thick end of the dough over the marzipan into the middle, and then fold the other end over into the middle. Fold the thicker half over the top of the remaining dough and seal the ends. Place on a baking sheet in a warm place until well risen.

**6** Bake in a preheated oven at 200°C, 400°F, Gas Mark 6 and, after 6-8 minutes, reduce the oven temperature to 170°C, 325°F, Gas Mark 3. Cover loosely with foil and bake for about 40 minutes or until cooked through and golden brown.

**7** Brush the hot stollen with melted butter and dust with icing sugar. Cool, then wrap in greaseproof paper and foil and store in an airtight container for 2 weeks before serving.

# APPLES IN PUFF PASTRY *with* CALVADOS BUTTER SAUCE

This is my all-time favourite dessert! The marriage of apples and Calvados is very old but I never tire of it.

### SERVES 4

75 g (3 oz) sultanas
2 tablespoons Calvados
4 Reinette apples or good dessert apples
pinch of ground cinnamon
300 g (10 oz) puff pastry
1 egg yolk, beaten
25 g (1 oz) icing sugar
50 g (2 oz) caster sugar
50 ml (2 fl oz) water
2 teaspoons glucose
50 g (2 oz) unsalted butter
150 ml (¼ pint) double cream

1 Soak the sultanas in the Calvados for at least 1 hour. Drain, reserving the Calvados. Top and tail the apples so that they stand level and remove the cores. Sprinkle the sultanas with cinnamon and use to fill the apples.

2 Roll out the puff pastry thinly. Cut out four ovals, about 17.5 cm (7 in) by 12.5 cm (5 in), and brush the edges with beaten egg yolk. Enclose an apple in each puff pastry oval, sealing the edges well and crimping with a small knife. Brush all over with egg yolk and make a small cut in the top.

3 Bake the apples in a preheated oven at 190°C, 375°F, Gas Mark 5 for about 20 minutes until golden

brown. Remove and dust generously with icing sugar. Place briefly under a hot grill to give a shiny glaze.

4 Meanwhile, put the sugar, water and glucose in a thick-based pan and stir over low heat until the sugar completely dissolves. Cook to a pale amber colour, then stir in the butter and cream, reserving 2 tablespoons for decoration. Stir in the Calvados, then pass the sauce through a fine sieve.

5 Place an apple on each serving plate and surround with the sauce. Feather it with the reserved cream.

*Wine: Riesling Spätlese 1992 (Germany)*

# SWEET PASTRY

### MAKES 675 G (1¹/₂ LB) PASTRY

*225 g (8 oz) softened butter*
*100 g (3¹/₂ oz) caster sugar*
*1 egg, lightly beaten*
*350 g (12 oz) flour*
*pinch of salt*

**1** Using a wooden spoon, cream the butter with the sugar until the mixture is smooth and very pale. Mix in the beaten egg.

**2** Add the flour and salt, a little at a time, slowly stirring into the creamed mixture. When it becomes too stiff to stir, continue mixing in the flour with your hands. Mix to a smooth ball.

**3** Wrap the dough in a polythene bag and leave to rest in the refrigerator for at least 2 hours before using.

# BRANDY SAUCE

This sauce should have a light consistency – if necessary, add some more milk.
It can be served with Christmas pudding and many other festive desserts.

### SERVES 4

*400 ml (14 fl oz) milk*
*50 g (2 oz) sugar*
*25 g (1 oz) cornflour*
*4 tablespoons brandy*

**1** Boil all but 2 tablespoons of the milk with the sugar, stirring well until dissolved. Blend the cornflour with the remaining milk and whisk into the hot milk over the heat.

**2** Bring back to the boil, remove from the heat and stir in the brandy.

# CHRISTMAS F.VE MENU

SERVES 4

*Black Forest Onion and
Smoked Bacon Tart*

WEHLENER, SONNENUCH RIESLING SPATLESE

(MOSEL) 1992

*Cream of Celeriac Perfumed
with Truffle Oil*

*Fillet of Venison
with Chestnuts*

CROZES HERMITAGE (P JABOULET AINE) 1992

*Minestrone Vegetables*

*Spätzle*

*Rumtopf Berries with
Vanilla Ice Cream*

MORSI DI LUCE (CANTINA FLORIO) 1992

# CHRISTMAS EVE MENU

This is my mother's classic menu for Christmas Eve (without the truffle oil). It took her all day to cook this dinner but it was much appreciated by my father. We children were more excited about our presents, which we opened after dinner on Christmas Eve. My mother used to start collecting the soft fruit from our garden for the rumtopf during the summer. By the way, this menu would make a great alternative Christmas Day lunch.

## BLACK FOREST ONION *and* SMOKED BACON TART

*250 g (9 oz) strong plain flour*
*90 g (3¹/₂ oz) wholemeal flour*
*15 g (¹/₂ oz) fresh yeast*
*1 teaspoon sugar*
*200 ml (7 fl oz) water*
*2 teaspoons caraway seeds*
*1 egg, beaten*
*75 ml (3 fl oz) crème fraîche*
*7 g (¹/₄ oz) salt*
*1 kg (2 lb) onions, finely chopped*
*10 g (¹/₃ oz) butter*
*200 g (7 oz) smoked streaky bacon rashers*
*salt and freshly ground black pepper*

1 Mix the flours in a large bowl and make a well in the centre. Crumble in the yeast and add the sugar and 4 tablespoons of the water. Mix with a little of the surrounding flour to a spongy texture. Cover the bowl with a cloth and leave to 'prove' in a warm place for about 30 minutes, until the 'sponge' has doubled in size.

2 Add the caraway seeds, 4 teaspoons of the crème fraîche, salt and the remaining water. Mix with a spoon, bringing in the flour from the sides, to form a smooth dough. Cover the bowl with a cloth and leave in a warm place for 30 minutes.

3 Meanwhile, sweat the onions in the butter over low heat without colouring. Allow to cool slightly and

then mix in the beaten egg and half of the remaining crème fraîche. Season to taste with salt and freshly ground black pepper.

4 Roll out the dough on a lightly floured surface to a thickness of 5 mm (¹/₄ inch). Grease a baking sheet and line with the dough. Brush lightly with a little water and then spread the onion mixture over the top. Cover lightly with the remaining crème fraîche and arrange the bacon rashers over the top.

5 Bake in a preheated oven at 220°C, 425°F, Gas Mark 7 for about 40-50 minutes, until the base is crisp and brown and the topping is golden. Serve hot cut into slices.

# CREAM OF CELERIAC PERFUMED *with* TRUFFLE OIL

*50 g (2 oz) butter*
*500 g (1 lb 2 oz) celeriac, peeled and chopped*
*200 ml (7 fl oz) white port*
*2 litres (3¹/₂ pints) strong chicken stock*
*¹/₄ teaspoon truffle oil*
*50 ml (2 fl oz) crème fraîche*
*salt and freshly ground black pepper*

1 Heat the butter in a large saucepan and add the celeriac. Cover the pan with a lid and leave to sweat for 10 minutes over gentle heat, taking care not to colour the celeriac. Add the white port, stirring well, and turn up the heat. Cook vigorously over high heat until the liquid reduces by half.

2 Add the chicken stock and seasoning. Liquidize in a blender, add the truffle oil and then pass through a sieve.

3 Reheat the soup over low heat, whisk in the crème fraîche and serve.

# SPATZLE

*400 g (14 oz) plain flour*
*6 eggs*
*5 teaspoons oil*
*pinch of ground nutmeg*
*40 g (1¹/₂ oz) butter*
*salt and pepper*

1 Combine the flour with the eggs, oil, nutmeg, salt and pepper. Mix well to form a very elastic dough, and then beat well with a wooden spoon until air bubbles develop. Spread a small amount of the paste on a thin wooden board.

2 Bring a large saucepan of lightly salted water to the boil. Add a dash of oil, and then quickly dip the whole board with the paste into the boiling water. Using a palette knife, quickly scrape small strips of the paste off the board into the boiling water. Cook for 1 minute and remove with a slotted spoon. Drain and refresh. Cook the remaining dough in the same way.

3 Melt the butter and toss the spätzle in it until warm. Season to taste and serve.

# FILLET OF VENISON *with* CHESTNUTS

*200 g (7 oz) venison bones, chopped*
*1 onion, chopped*
*1 carrot, chopped*
*1 leek, chopped (outside leaves removed)*
*$^1$/2 tablespoon tomato purée*
*100 ml (3$^1$/2 fl oz) red wine*
*500 ml (18 fl oz) chicken stock*
*$^1$/2 teaspoon black peppercorns*
*2 juniper berries*
*few sprigs of thyme*
*600 g (1$^1$/4 lb) loin of venison, cut off the saddle*
*1 teaspoon mixed fresh herbs (finely chopped thyme, rosemary, marjoram)*
*2 tablespoons vegetable oil*
*450 g (1 lb) chestnuts*
*100 g (3$^1$/2 oz) unsalted butter*
*400 g (14 oz) Minestrone Vegetables (see opposite)*
*salt and pepper*

1 Heat a thick-based pan and roast the venison bones over medium heat until coloured. Add the onion, carrot and leek and cook for a further minute. Add the tomato purée and red wine, turn up the heat and reduce the liquid until the bones start to caramelize. Add the chicken stock, peppercorns, juniper berries and thyme, and simmer for 40 minutes. Pass through a fine sieve, return to the pan and boil until reduced by half.

2 Season the venison with salt and pepper and sprinkle with three-quarters of the mixed fresh herbs. Sear in hot oil in a pan, turning to seal in all the juices. Wrap the venison in foil and roast in a preheated oven at 220°C, 425°F, Gas Mark 7 for 6-8 minutes. Leave it a little longer if you prefer your meat to be more well cooked. Remove from the oven and set aside to 'rest' for 10 minutes.

3 Make a small incision in each chestnut with a sharp knife and then blanch them in boiling water. Drain and peel them. Sauté the chestnuts with the fennel seeds in a little of the butter. Set aside.

4 Heat the Minestrone Vegetables in a little butter and season with salt and pepper. Arrange them in a ring on each serving plate. Cut the venison into 5-mm (1/4-in) thick slices and fan out on top of the vegetables. Arrange 4 chestnuts around the vegetables.

5 Whisk the remaining butter into the sauce and pour a little over the venison. Sprinkle with the remaining mixed herbs and serve with spätzle (see recipe, page 73).

# RUMTOPF BERRIES

*100 ml (3¹/₂ fl oz) stock sugar syrup (see page 65)*
*50 ml (2 fl oz) dark rum*
*100 g (3¹/₂ oz) strawberries, hulled*
*100 g (3¹/₂ oz) raspberries*
*100 g (3¹/₂ oz) blueberries*
*100 g (3¹/₂ oz) blackberries*
*100 g (3¹/₂ oz) black cherries, stoned*
*vanilla ice cream, to serve*

**1** Mix the stock sugar syrup with the rum and pour into an earthenware pot. Wash the fruit and arrange in layers in the pot. This can be done throughout the summer months as they ripen. Seal or cover the pot and store in a cool dark place until Christmas.

**2** To serve the rumtopf, warm the fruit gently and transfer to serving bowls. Top each one with a quenelle of vanilla ice cream.

# MINESTRONE VEGETABLES

*3 carrots, cut into 1-cm (¹/₂-in) squares*
*2 leeks, trimmed and cut into 1-cm (¹/₂-in) squares*
*50 g (2 oz) broccoli florets*
*50 g (2 oz) shelled broad beans*
*25 g (1 oz) butter*
*75 g (3 oz) wild mushrooms (e.g. girolles, cèpes, oyster mushrooms), blanched*
*25 g (1 oz) freshly grated Parmesan cheese*
*salt and freshly ground black pepper*

**1** Cook the carrots and leeks separately in salted boiling water until just tender. Drain and refresh. Cook the broccoli and broad beans in the same way, reserving a little of the cooking water.

**2** Heat the butter in a large pan, add the mushrooms and cook gently for 2-3 minutes. Add the rest of the vegetables and toss gently in the melted butter.

**3** Add a little of the reserved cooking liquid and cook gently until the liquid evaporates. Season to taste with salt and pepper and then sprinkle with Parmesan.

# CHRISTMAS DAY MENU

SERVES 4

*Sea Bass Topped with Candied Vegetables*

CHARDONNAY, STELLENRYCK (SOUTH AFRICA)

*Roast Goose with Apple and Prune Stuffing*

CALITERRA, CABERNET SAUVIGNON (CHILE)

*Fried Potatoes with Garlic and Rosemary*

*Brussels Sprouts*

*Mrs Wood's Christmas Pudding*

ESSENCIA, ORANGE MUSCAT (CALIFORNIA)

# CHRISTMAS DAY MENU

This menu is very much in keeping with Christmas: a light and elegant starter followed by two traditional dishes. If wished, the goose could be served with Braised Red Cabbage with Prunes (see page 52) and Baked Chicory (see page 53).

## SEA BASS TOPPED *with* CANDIED VEGETABLES

This is a light and delicious way to start your Christmas meal. You could substitute John Dory or less expensive trout fillets for the sea bass, if wished.

*1/2 red pepper, seeded and diced*
*1/2 green pepper, seeded and diced*
*skin of 1 aubergine, diced*
*skin of 1 courgette, diced*
*150 g (5 oz) sugar*
*1 tablespoon sherry vinegar*
*4 x 150 g (5 oz) fillets of sea bass*
*3 tablespoons olive oil*
*juice of 1/2 lemon*
*4 tablespoons chopped fresh chives*
*salt and freshly ground black pepper*

1 Blanch the red and green peppers with the skin of the aubergine and courgette in boiling water. Refresh in iced water and drain well.

2 Make the stock syrup with 250 ml (8 fl oz) water and the sugar. Stir over low heat until the sugar has dissolved and then boil until slightly thickened and syrupy. Add the drained vegetables to the syrup, transfer to a baking dish and cook in a preheated oven at 160°C, 325°F, Gas Mark 3 for 30 minutes.

3 Meanwhile, wash and dry the sea bass fillets and season them with salt and pepper. Heat the olive oil and fry the fillets, skin side down, until the skin is very crisp. Turn them over, add the lemon juice and cook for 1 minute, until the flesh is opaque and translucent.

4 Transfer the fish to four serving plates and surround with the vegetables. Sprinkle with chopped chives.

# ROAST GOOSE *with* APPLE *and* PRUNE STUFFING

Before turkey was widely available, goose was the traditional dish for Christmas Day; it still is in central Europe.
To prevent it being fatty, pour off the fat frequently while the goose is cooking and roast it until crisp.

*1 apple, cored and chopped*
*2 onions, chopped*
*2 sprigs of sage*
*1 x 3.5 kg (6$^1/_2$ lb) goose, with giblets and trimmings (winglets etc.)*
*1 garlic clove, crushed*
*1 carrot, sliced*
*1 tablespoon tomato purée*
*$^1/_2$ bay leaf*
*$^1/_4$ teaspoon black peppercorns, crushed*
*100 ml (3$^1/_2$ fl oz) port*
*1 litre (1 pint 18 fl oz) strong chicken stock*
*$^1/_4$ loaf white bread, crusts removed*
*150 g (5 oz) clarified butter*
*450 g (1 lb) apples, peeled, cored and cut into 5-mm ($^1/_4$-in) thick slices*
*300 g (10 oz) prunes, soaked in cold tea and squeezed*
*salt and pepper*

**1** Mix the apple with one of the chopped onions and the sage. Place inside the empty cavity of the goose. Season generously with salt and pepper. Pour cold water into a large roasting pan to a depth of 5 mm ($^1/_4$ in) and place the goose in it lying on one side.

**2** Roast in a preheated oven at 180°C, 350°F, Gas Mark 4 for 30 minutes, then turn the goose over on to its other side. After a further 30 minutes, remove from the oven and drain off the fat. Turn the goose on to its back and roast for 1 hour, basting frequently, until cooked. Remove from the pan and rest in a warm place.

**3** While the goose is roasting, brown the goose liver and other giblets and trimmings in a little fat. Add the remaining onion, garlic and carrot and roast for 5 minutes. Stir in the tomato purée, bay leaf and crushed peppercorns and fry on top of the stove for 2-3 minutes, until the tomato purée caramelizes. Add the port and stock, and simmer for 30 minutes, skimming frequently. Pass the gravy through a fine sieve, return to the pan and continue cooking until reduced to the desired consistency.

**4** Cut the bread into 1-cm ($^1/_2$-in) croûtons and fry gently in three-quarters of the clarified butter until golden brown all over. Drain on kitchen paper. Sauté the apple slices gently in the remaining butter until tender. Add the drained prunes and heat through. At the last minute, add the bread croûtons.

**5** Carve the goose and serve with the apple and prune stuffing and the gravy.

# FRIED POTATOES *with* GARLIC *and* ROSEMARY

*900 g (2 lb) potatoes, peeled*
*100 ml (3¹/₂ fl oz) vegetable oil*
*1 garlic clove, peeled and halved*
*25 g (1 oz) unsalted butter*
*2 sprigs of rosemary, crumbled*
*salt and freshly ground black pepper*

**1** Cut the potatoes into quarters or trim them into 'barrel' shapes, 5 cm (2 in) long and 2.5 cm (1 in) wide. Heat the oil in a non-stick pan which is just large enough to hold the potatoes in a single layer. Add the potatoes and garlic, cover the pan and cook gently for 30 minutes, without letting them colour too much.

**2** When the potatoes are nearly soft, add the butter and rosemary and turn up the heat to colour the potatoes golden brown. Season the potatoes to taste with salt and freshly ground black pepper and then drain on absorbent kitchen paper. Transfer to a serving dish and keep warm.

---

*CHRISTMAS NIBBLES*

# CHEESE SABLES

### MAKES 40

*225 g (8 oz) plain flour*
*1 teaspoon mustard powder*
*225 g (8 oz) unsalted butter*
*225 g (8 oz) mature Cheddar cheese, grated*
*salt and freshly ground black pepper*
*beaten egg, to glaze*
*poppy seeds, to sprinkle*

#### For the filling:
*100 g (3¹/₂ oz) mature Cheddar cheese, grated*
*100 g (3¹/₂ oz) curd cheese*
*1 teaspoon Dijon mustard*
*¹/₂ teaspoon paprika*
*1-2 tablespoons milk*

**1** Sift the flour and mustard powder together. Rub in the butter, then add the cheese and season with salt and pepper. Work the mixture together to form a firm dough.

**2** Roll out on a lightly floured surface and cut out 80 rounds, 1 cm (¹/₂ in) in diameter. Place the rounds on baking trays and then chill in the refrigerator for at least 20 minutes.

**3** Brush 40 rounds with beaten egg and sprinkle with poppy seeds. Bake in a preheated oven at 190°C, 375°F, Gas Mark 5 for 12-15 minutes, until golden brown. Cool on a wire tray.

**4** Beat the filling ingredients together in a bowl and use to sandwich the pastry rounds together, using the poppy seeded rounds for the tops. Serve as nibbles with drinks.

# MRS WOOD'S CHRISTMAS PUDDING

Our Christmas pudding is always supplied by Mrs Wood, an old family friend. She is eighty-two years old and joins us with her family for Christmas every year. She prepares the pudding in August and wraps it in a hand-crocheted Christmas pudding cosy. Everyone who tastes it agrees that this pudding is simply the best!

*115 g (4 oz) shredded suet*
*50 g (2 oz) self-raising flour*
*115 g (4 oz) white breadcrumbs*
*1 level teaspoon ground mixed spice*
*1/4 teaspoon grated nutmeg*
*good pinch of ground cinnamon*
*250 g (9 oz) dark brown soft sugar*
*550 g (1 1/4 lb) mixed dried fruit (currants, sultanas, raisins)*
*25 g (1 oz) mixed candied peel*
*25 g (1 oz) chopped almonds*
*1 small cooking apple, peeled, cored and finely chopped*
*grated zest of 1/2 large orange*
*grated zest of 1/2 large lemon*
*150 ml (1/4 pint) stout*
*75 ml (3 fl oz) rum or brandy*
*2 large eggs*

**1** Put the suet, flour, breadcrumbs, spices and sugar in a large bowl, and mix well. Gradually stir in the mixed fruit, candied peel, nuts, apple, orange and lemon zest.

**2** Measure the stout into another bowl. Add the rum or brandy and beat in the eggs. Pour this mixture into the large bowl and mix thoroughly until the pudding mixture is fairly sloppy. Cover the bowl and leave it to stand overnight.

**3** The following day, fill a lightly greased 1.1-litre (2-pint) pudding basin with the mixture. Cover with a double thickness of greaseproof paper and some aluminium foil, and tie securely with string.

**4** Place the pudding basin on an upturned saucer in a large pan of simmering water which comes halfway up the sides. Cook for 7-8 hours, topping up the water occasionally to the right level and taking care that it does not boil dry. Alternatively, cook in the top of a steamer.

**5** Leave the pudding to go cold and then remove the covers and replace with fresh ones. Store in a cool, dry place until Christmas Day. To reheat, steam the pudding for 2 hours. Serve with brandy and cream.

# FESTIVE VEGETARIAN MENU

SERVES 4

Red Pepper and Wild
Mushroom Salad with
Garlic Croûtons

SANCERRE (A DEZAT) 1994 (LOIRE)

Cappuccino of Pumpkin
and Coriander

Vegetable Cannelloni with
Walnut Sauce

ROCATTO, CABERNET SAUVIGNON
(ROCCA DELLE MARCIE) 1990 (ITALY)

Vodka Sorbet Pavlova
with Exotic Fruit

ESSENCIA, BLACK MUSCAT (CALIFORNIA)

# FESTIVE VEGETARIAN MENU

After a marathon of food and drink over the Christmas holidays, I think that even non-vegetarians should consider serving a menu such as this and give their digestive systems an easy, restful day.

## RED PEPPER *and* WILD MUSHROOM SALAD *with* GARLIC CROUTONS

*6 red peppers*
*10 garlic cloves, peeled*
*200 g (7 oz) wild mushrooms (e.g. shitaki, cèpes, girolles etc.)*
*1/2 bread flute (small baguette)*
*200 ml (7 fl oz) olive oil*
*3 sprigs of rosemary*
*100 ml (3 1/2 fl oz) balsamic vinegar*
*juice of 1/2 lemon*
*115 g (4 oz) mixed salad leaves*
*salt and pepper*

1 Put the red peppers on the grill pan and place under a preheated grill, turning them occasionally, until the skin blackens and blisters all over. Remove the peppers and place them in a paper bag for a few minutes. Peel them, removing the stalks, ribs and seeds, and then cut the flesh into squares.

2 Dip the garlic cloves into boiling water for 30 seconds. Remove them and repeat twice. Cut the garlic into thin slices. Blanch the mushrooms in the same way and cut into slices.

3 Cut the French bread into 5-mm (1/4-inch) thick slices, brush with a little of the olive oil and toast on both sides. Top them with three-quarters of the sliced garlic.

4 Heat a little of the remaining olive oil in a pan and gently fry the remaining garlic and rosemary until the garlic is soft and the rosemary has infused the oil. Add the mushrooms and red peppers, and simmer for 10 minutes. Season and stir in half of the balsamic vinegar.

5 Mix 100 ml (3 1/2 fl oz) of the olive oil with the lemon juice and a little salt and pepper. Toss the salad leaves in this dressing and arrange on serving plates. Place the red pepper and mushroom mixture in the centre.

6 Reheat the garlic croûtons under the grill and divide between the serving plates. Sprinkle the remaining balsamic vinegar over the top.

# CAPPUCCINO OF PUMPKIN *and* CORIANDER

*75 g (3 oz) chopped onion*
*40 g (1¹/₂ oz) butter*
*2 tablespoons groundnut oil*
*800 g (1³/₄ lb) pumpkin, skin removed and cut into dice*
*75 g (3 oz) chopped leek*
*600 ml (1 pint) chicken stock*
*400 ml (14 fl oz) milk*
*10 sprigs of coriander, stalks reserved and leaves finely chopped*
*salt and pepper*

1 Cook the onion gently in the butter and groundnut oil until soft and translucent. Add the pumpkin and leek, cover the pan and continue cooking over low heat until soft. Add the chicken stock, milk and coriander stalks, and season with salt and pepper. Simmer gently for 20 minutes.

2 Liquidize the soup in a blender or food processor and pass through a fine sieve. Return to the pan and add the chopped coriander leaves. Reheat gently and use an electric hand liquidizer to make the soup foamy.

# VEGETABLE CANNELLONI *with* WALNUT SAUCE

*300 g (10 oz) pasta dough (see below)*
*3 garlic cloves, crushed*
*4 tablespoons olive oil*
*300 g (10 oz) spinach, trimmed, blanched and roughly chopped*
*300 g (10 oz) ricotta cheese*
*25 g (1 oz) freshly grated Parmesan cheese*
*2 eggs, beaten*
*pinch of ground nutmeg*
*12 chives, blanched and refreshed*
*50 g (2 oz) finely chopped onion*
*100 g (3¹/2 oz) walnuts*
*25 g (1 oz) pine nuts*
*100 ml (3¹/2 fl oz) dry white wine*
*200 ml (7 fl oz) vegetable stock*
*200 ml (7 fl oz) double cream*
*salt and pepper*
*sprigs of oregano, to garnish*

**1** Roll out the pasta thinly using setting No. 1 on a pasta machine, if you have one. Cut the pasta into eight 12-cm (5-in) squares. Blanch them in boiling salted water, refresh and drain.

**2** Gently sweat 2 crushed garlic cloves in some of the olive oil and then add the spinach, ricotta, Parmesan and eggs. Season with salt and pepper and nutmeg and remove from the heat.

**3** Place a little of the spinach mixture on one of the pasta sheets and roll up tightly like a cracker. Tie each end with one of the blanched chives, and brush with a little olive oil to prevent the pasta drying out. Repeat with the remaining pasta squares.

**4** Cook the onions until soft and translucent in the rest of the olive oil. Add the remaining garlic clove and cook gently for 1 minute. Stir in three-quarters of the walnuts and pine nuts together with the white wine. Turn up the heat and reduce the sauce by half. Add the vegetable stock and cream, and cook until slightly reduced and thickened. Liquidize and season to taste.

**5** Place the cannelloni in the top of a steamer over simmering water and steam for 6 minutes. Arrange on 4 serving plates and pour the sauce around them. Garnish with the reserved walnuts, pine nuts and sprigs of fresh oregano.

## PASTA DOUGH

*225 g (8 oz) plain flour*
*2 eggs*
*1 egg yolk*
*¹/2 teaspoon salt*
*¹/2 tablespoon extra virgin olive oil*

Combine all the ingredients together in a food processor to make a firm, smooth dough. Alternatively, mix them with your hands.

# VODKA SORBET PAVLOVA *with* EXOTIC FRUIT

*225 g (8 oz) caster sugar*
*4 egg whites*

**For the sorbet:**
*350 ml (12 fl oz) water*
*200 g (7 oz) sugar*
*50 ml (2 fl oz) glucose syrup*
*1 tablespoon lemon juice*
*75 ml (3 fl oz) vodka*

**For the exotic fruit:**
*1 mango, peeled, stoned and diced*
*1 papaya, peeled and diced*
*2 kiwi fruit, peeled and diced*
*50 g (2 oz) strawberries, hulled and diced*
*4 sprigs of mint, to garnish*

**1** Make the meringue. Spread the caster sugar out on a baking tray lined with greaseproof paper and place in a preheated oven at 200°C, 400°F, Gas Mark 6 until the sugar is hot to the touch.

**2** Whip the egg whites until they form soft peaks. Remove the hot sugar from the oven and whisk into the egg whites, a little at a time. Continue whisking the meringue until it is cold. Spoon the meringue into a piping bag and pipe eight 7.5-cm (3-in) circles, about 5 mm (1/4 in) thick, on two baking trays lined with baking parchment. Place in a cool oven at 130°C, 250°F, Gas Mark 1/2 for approximately 3 hours, until the meringues are crisp and dry.

**3** To make the sorbet, boil the water, sugar, glucose syrup, lemon juice and vodka together and then freeze in a sorbet machine, or pour into a freezing container and place in the freezer. Remove occasionally, stir well and replace in the freezer, until frozen.

**4** With a round pastry cutter, cut out four 7.5-cm (3-in) circles of sorbet and place on top of four meringue circles. Cover with the remaining meringue discs. Carefully place them in the freezer and leave for at least 30 minutes.

**5** Mix all the diced fruit together. Reserve a little for decorating the meringues, and spread out the remainder in 10-cm (4-in) circles on four dessert plates. Place a meringue in the centre of each fruit ring, and spoon a little of the reserved fruit on top. Decorate with tiny sprigs of mint and serve immediately.

# BOXING DAY MENU

SERVES 4

*Bayonne Ham with Marinated Mushrooms*

MUSCAT (SCHLUMBERGER) 1993 (ALSACE)

*Tournedos of Turbot with Pesto Sauce*

BAROLO, DE SERRALUNGA D'ALBA
(FONTANAFREDDA) 1991 (ITALY)

*New Potatoes in their Skins*

*Green vegetable or salad*

*Warm Figs with Crème Fraîche*

CHATEAU FILHOT (SAUTERNES) 1988

This menu is quickly executed, light and fresh. Indeed, it is perfect for revitalizing you after the spoils of Christmas and a well-earned rest for the cook! Most of it can be prepared in advance before the holidays, including the pesto sauce, artichokes and marinated mushrooms. On the day, all you need is basic assembly time.

# BAYONNE HAM *with* MARINATED MUSHROOMS

*50 ml (2 fl oz) wine vinegar*
*300 g (10 oz) pine mushrooms (or shitake), washed and halved*
*250 ml (8 fl oz) olive oil (first cold pressing)*
*sprigs of fresh basil, tarragon, thyme, rosemary*
*¹/₂ teaspoon white pepper*
*1 tablespoon sea salt*
*225 g (8 oz) Bayonne ham, sliced very thinly*

1 Put the vinegar in a saucepan with 500 ml (18 fl oz) water and bring to the boil. Add the mushrooms and boil for 2 minutes. Remove the mushrooms and drain them well. Dry on absorbent kitchen paper.

2 Place the drained mushrooms in a clay pot, and pour the olive oil over the top. Add the fresh herbs, and season with white pepper and sea salt. Cover with a lid and leave to marinate for 48 hours.

3 To serve, place the marinated mushrooms on four serving plates and then cover them with very thinly sliced Bayonne ham.

# BRANDY BUTTER

*115 g (4 oz) unsalted butter*
*115 g (4 oz) caster sugar*
*3 tablespoons brandy*

1 Cream the butter until pale, then beat in the sugar, a little at a time, until well blended and creamy. Beat in the brandy, a few drops at a time, taking care that it does not curdle.

2 Put the Brandy Butter in a bowl and chill in the refrigerator. Serve it with Christmas pudding or mince pies.

# TOURNEDOS OF TURBOT *with* PESTO SAUCE

*4 baby artichokes*
*2 tablespoons olive oil*
*400 g (14 oz) turbot fillet, skinned and boned*
*2 tablespoons chopped fresh parsley*
*150 g (5 oz) baby courgettes, trimmed, blanched and thinly sliced*
*6 tablespoons Light Pesto Sauce (see below)*
*4 plum tomatoes, skinned, seeded and cut into strips*
*salt and pepper*
*few sprigs of chervil, to garnish*

1 Remove the stalks and outside leaves from the artichokes and slice them finely. Sauté in half of the olive oil until tender. Season with salt and pepper, and set aside to cool.

2 Cut the turbot into 12 thin slices and season with salt and pepper. Place one slice on a piece of clingfilm and cover with 1/2 tablespoon of the artichokes and a little parsley. Place a second slice of turbot on top and cover with some more artichokes and parsley. Top this with a third slice of turbot. Repeat this with the remaining turbot, artichokes and parsley so that you have four turbot tournedos.

3 Season the sliced courgettes and lay them over the fish, overlapping each other. Wrap each tournedos in cling film and then place in the top of a steamer over simmering water for 8 minutes.

4 Heat the Light Pesto Sauce and spread some in a large circle in the centre of each serving plate. Heat the tomatoes in the remaining olive oil, season with salt and pepper and arrange around the pesto. Unwrap the turbot tournedos and place in the centre of the pesto. Brush with a little olive oil and garnish with sprigs of chervil.

## LIGHT PESTO SAUCE

*75 g (3 oz) basil leaves*
*40 g (1 1/2 oz) pine nuts*
*130 ml (4 1/2 fl oz) extra virgin olive oil*
*salt and pepper*

Place all the ingredients in a food processor or blender and liquidize until you have a green purée.

# WARM FIGS *with* CREME FRAICHE

*400 ml (14 fl oz) port*
*225 g (8 oz) granulated sugar*
*pared rind of 2 lemons*
*2 cinnamon sticks*
*16 small fresh figs*
*4 clementines, peeled*
*ground cinnamon, for dusting*
*crème fraîche, to serve*

**1** Put the port, sugar, lemon rind and cinnamon sticks in a saucepan with 150 ml (¼ pint) water. Heat gently, stirring over the heat until the sugar has completely dissolved. Turn up the heat, bring to the boil and then boil rapidly until reduced by half and syrupy.

**2** Add the figs and clementines to the syrup, cover the pan and poach gently for 6-8 minutes until tender.

Carefully transfer the poached fruit to a pretty serving dish, using a slotted spoon.

**3** Remove the lemon rind and cinnamon sticks from the syrup and then boil it rapidly until reduced by half. Pour over the fruit. Serve lukewarm dusted with ground cinnamon. Serve the crème fraîche on the side.

# CHRISTMAS COCKTAILS

## SANTA'S TIPPLE

*one-fifth Bacardi rum*
*one-fifth Mandarine Napoleon*
*three-fifths mandarin juice*
*3 dashes Frangelico*
*3 dashes rose water*
*1 egg white*
*Cape gooseberries (physalis), to decorate*

Shake all the ingredients together, pour into a glass and decorate with Cape gooseberries (physalis).

## REINDEER NECTAR

*two-fifths cranberry sauce*
*two-fifths apple juice*
*one-fifth mango juice*
*4 strawberries*
*1 slice of melon, rind removed*
*melon chunks and cherries, to decorate*

Put the fruit juices, strawberries and melon in a blender, and blend together. Pour into a glass and decorate with melon and cherries.

# New year's eve menu

### Serves 4

---

*Celebration Lobster*

GAVI (PIO CESARE) 1994 (ITALY)

---

*Warm Potato Salad with Chives and Caviar*

---

*Breast of Guinea Fowl with Caramelized Onions*

CHATEAUNEUF DU PAPE (DOMAINE DU VIEUX TELEGRAPHE) 1993 (RHONE)

---

*Spinach with Cream and Cumin*

---

*Banana and Ginger Soufflé with Mango Sauce*

MUMM, CORDON VERT, RICH

# NEW YEAR'S EVE MENU

New Year's Eve menus should be luxurious and abundant, and how better to express this than with the food and wine you serve on this special occasion? Whereas Christmas food is traditional, tonight's menu symbolizes the creative flair and optimism which are symbolic of the New Year celebrations.

## CELEBRATION LOBSTER

*4 x 450 g (1 lb) cooked lobsters*
*3 tablespoons olive oil*
*25 g (1 oz) baby spinach, trimmed and washed*
*50 g (2 oz) walnuts, roughly chopped*
*1 pomegranate, halved*
*1 tablespoon lemon juice*
*15 g (1/2 oz) lamb's lettuce, washed*
*salt and pepper*

1 Remove the shells from the lobsters. Start by twisting off the two large claws, and then twist again at the first joint to separate them from the knuckles. Twist the head to separate it from the tail. Lay the tail on its side and press down firmly to crack the undershell. Carefully peel away the shell and cut the meat into angled slices.

2 Heat 1 tablespoon of the oil in a non-stick frying pan and add the sliced lobster, spinach and walnuts. Scoop the bright red seeds out of the pomegranate and add to the pan. Mix the remaining olive oil with the lemon juice and a little salt and pepper, and stir two-thirds of this into the lobster mixture.

3 Mix the lamb's lettuce with the remaining oil and lemon juice dressing and then arrange in a ring on each serving plate. Place the warm lobster mixture in the centre and garnish with the reserved claws and legs.

# WARM POTATO SALAD *with* CHIVES *and* CAVIAR

*600 g (1¼ lb) small new potatoes*
*100 ml (3½ fl oz) crème fraîche or sour cream*
*2 tablespoons mayonnaise*
*2 tablespoons chopped fresh chives*
*50 g (2 oz) caviar, preferably Ocietra or Sevruga*
*4 small handfuls of lamb's lettuce*
*salt and pepper*

**For the sherry vinaigrette:**
*1 tablespoon olive oil*
*1 teaspoon sherry vinegar*
*salt and freshly ground black pepper*

**1** Boil the potatoes in lightly salted water for 10-15 minutes, until they are just tender. Drain and set aside to cool a little. When they are hot enough to handle, peel the potatoes, cut them into 5-mm (¼-in) slices and keep warm.

**2** In a large bowl, combine the crème fraîche, mayonnaise and chives, and season with salt and pepper. Add the potatoes and fold into the mixture. Add three-quarters of the caviar and mix very gently. Transfer to a serving bowl or four individual serving plates and top with the remaining caviar.

**3** Whisk the vinaigrette ingredients together and use to toss the lamb's lettuce. Arrange the lamb's lettuce around the potato salad and serve immediately.

# SPINACH *with* CREAM AND CUMIN

*600 g (1¼ lb) young spinach leaves*
*50 ml (2 fl oz) olive oil*
*25 g (1 oz) butter*
*25 g (1 oz) finely chopped shallots or onions*
*1 garlic clove, crushed*
*100 ml (3½ fl oz) thick double cream*
*salt and pepper and a good pinch of cumin*

**1** Pick the spinach over, removing any thick stems, and wash the leaves three times. Drain well.

**2** Heat half of the oil and add the spinach. Cook rapidly, stirring, until the leaves are limp. Remove, cool slightly and press out the liquid with a saucer in a sieve.

**3** Heat the remaining oil and the butter and add the shallots or onions. Cook gently until soft and translucent. Add the garlic and cook for 1 more minute. Add the spinach and cream and season to taste with salt and pepper and a pinch of cumin.

# BREAST OF GUINEA FOWL
## *with* CARAMELIZED ONIONS

*4 x 150 g (5 oz) guinea fowl breasts*
*100 ml (3<sup>1</sup>/2 fl oz) olive oil*
*2 onions, finely chopped*
*3 garlic cloves, crushed*
*1/2 leek, trimmed and diced*
*1/2 celery head, diced*
*1 large carrot, diced*
*25 g (1 oz) sugar*
*200 ml (7 fl oz) balsamic vinegar*
*500 ml (18 fl oz) chicken stock*
*24 button onions, peeled*
*115 g (4 oz) plum tomatoes, skinned, seeded and diced*
*few sprigs of sage, finely chopped*
*75 g (3 oz) unsalted butter, softened*
*salt and pepper*

1 Season the guinea fowl with salt and pepper, and then sauté gently in half of the olive oil until golden brown. Remove from the pan and keep warm. Add the chopped onions and cook gently until soft and translucent. Add the garlic and cook for 1 minute. Stir in the leek, celery, carrot, sugar and balsamic vinegar. Turn up the heat and bubble gently until reduced by half. Add the chicken stock and reduce again to half its original volume. Return the guinea fowl to the pan and place in a preheated oven at 200°C, 400°F, Gas Mark 6 for 7 minutes.

2 Heat the remaining oil in a heavy-based flameproof casserole. Add the button onions; they should fit in a single layer. Sauté them quickly to colour them, turning occasionally. Season with salt and pepper, then cover the casserole and cook in the oven until tender but still firm (about 10-15 minutes).

3 Remove the guinea fowl from the pan and keep warm. Add the tomatoes to the pan and place over medium heat to reduce the sauce and thicken it slightly. Stir in the sage and work in the butter. Season to taste with salt and pepper.

4 Serve the guinea fowl breasts with the sauce, garnished with the button onions.

# BANANA *and* GINGER SOUFFLE
# *with* MANGO SAUCE

*15 g (¹/₂ oz) caster sugar*
*115 g (4 oz) banana purée*
*2 teaspoons cornflour*
*1 egg yolk*
*2 knobs candied stem ginger, chopped*
*2 egg whites*
*15 g (¹/₂ oz) icing sugar*
*¹/₂ banana, thinly sliced*


**For the mango sauce:**
*1 tablespoon Amaretto liqueur*
*100 g (3¹/₂ oz) mango purée*
*25 g (1 oz) passion fruit purée*
*25 g (1 oz) sugar*
*1 teaspoon cornflour*


**For decoration:**
*icing sugar, for dusting*
*1 mango, thinly sliced*

**1** Butter four 6-cm (2¹/₂-in) soufflé dishes and pour in a little of the caster sugar to coat the sides and base. Put the remaining sugar in a pan with the banana purée and bring to the boil. Mix a teaspoon of cornflour with a little water and stir into the banana purée to thicken it. Remove from the heat and stir in the egg yolks and ginger.

**2** Whip the egg whites with the remaining cornflour and the icing sugar until they form stiff peaks. Fold gently into the banana purée. Place three slices of banana in each soufflé dish and then fill with the banana mixture. Stand in a bain-marie or a roasting pan with water halfway up the sides of the dishes. Cook in a preheated oven at 220°C, 425°F, Gas Mark 7 for 20 minutes.

**3** Meanwhile, make the mango sauce. Mix the Amaretto, mango and passion fruit purées, and sugar in a saucepan, and bring to the boil. Blend the cornflour with a little water, and then stir into the sauce. Continue stirring until slightly thickened, then remove from the heat and cool.

**4** Pour the sauce into four serving dishes or soup plates. Turn out the soufflés and place one on each dish. Dust with icing sugar and decorate with sliced mango.

# CHRISTMAS DRINKS

When the cold winter evenings begin to draw in and the need to warm the spirit of friends and family is thrust upon you, then it's good to have a selection of winter drinks close at hand. This is especially important at Christmas when you have guests and friends drop in to wish you well.

### CHRISTMAS PARTY DRINKS

Every Christmas party should begin with Hot Egg Nog, a truly English warming drink. This wonderful concoction, served in a highball glass, consists of brandy and rum in equal parts, mixed with an egg and then stirred and topped up with hot milk and freshly grated nutmeg.

Before dinner, it is still traditional to offer your guests a glass of Sherry. The word 'Sherry', which is anglicized from the Spanish Jerez, refers to the fortified wine produced in that region of Spain since the sixteenth century.

After dinner, we should still make time to enjoy the wonders of a fine Madeira. This sweet wine is not normally cloying but is quite dry in taste, and was traditionally eaten with rich fruit cakes and, of course, Madeira cake.

This is also a good time to enjoy a glass of Port. Late-bottled vintage Port from Taylors or a vintage Port from one of the great houses, such as Grahams, is a delightful way to finish the perfect Christmas meal and warm you up before venturing out into a cold winter's night.

### MULLED WINES

Mulled wines, such as Christmas Cheer and Magic Punch, make warming, seasonal drinks. Basically, they are hot wines to which sugar and spices are added. Brandy and fortified wines may also be added for extra strength and flavour. Although they should always be served very hot, they should never be boiled or the alcohol will evaporate. Nor should you use expensive wines — simple, inexpensive ones are very good and far more economical.

# CHRISTMAS CHEER

### MAKES 30 GLASSES

*4 bottles of red wine*
*600 ml (1 pint) water*
*¹/₂ bottle dark rum*
*1 lemon*
*12 cloves*
*¹/₂ teaspoon ground cinnamon*
*freshly grated nutmeg*

**1** Heat the wine, water and rum in a large saucepan. Stick the lemon with the cloves and bake in a preheated oven at 180°C, 350°F, Gas Mark 4 for 15 minutes.

**2** Sprinkle the cinnamon and nutmeg over the wine mixture and float the hot lemon on the top. Serve hot in wine glasses.

# MAGIC PUNCH

This is traditionally made with a sugar cone placed in a holder over the saucepan of punch. Warmed rum is poured over the cone and set alight, gradually melting the sugar into the wine below. You can substitute sugar cubes as described below.

### MAKES 12 GLASSES

*3 bottles of red wine*
*2 cloves*
*12.5 cm (5 inches) cinnamon stick*
*grated rind and juice of 1 lemon*
*juice of 2 oranges*
*250 g (9 oz) sugar cubes*
*600 ml (1 pint) dark rum*

**1** Put the wine, spices and grated lemon rind into a large saucepan and heat gently. Stir in the lemon and orange juices. Pack the sugar cubes into a stainless steel sieve and set it across the top of the saucepan.

**2** Warm the rum and gradually pour some of it over the sugar. Set fire to it, adding more rum from time to time to keep the flames alight. When all the sugar has melted into the punch, stir well and serve.

**FESTIVE TIP:** To prevent your wine glass from cracking when serving hot mulled wine, pour the wine over a spoon into the glass.

# PAILLETTES *aux* HERBES

### MAKES: 50

*250 g (9 oz) puff pastry*
*1 egg, beaten, to glaze*
*50 g (2 oz) grated Parmesan cheese*
*1¹/₂ teaspoons chopped fresh rosemary*
*1¹/₂ teaspoons chopped fresh sage*
*1 teaspoon paprika*
*2 teaspoons caraway seeds*

**1** Roll out the pastry, about 3 mm (¹/₈ in) thick, on a lightly floured surface. Cut into three equal portions, brush with beaten egg and sprinkle with Parmesan cheese. Sprinkle one portion with herbs, one with paprika and one with caraway seeds.

**2** Fold each portion over and then roll out again to 3 mm (¹/₈ in) thick. Cut into strips, about 15 cm (6 in) long and 5 mm (¹/₄ in) wide. Roll each strip with your hands to achieve a twisted effect. Leave to rest in a cool place for at least 20 minutes.

**3** Bake the paillettes on lightly greased baking trays in a preheated oven at 200°C, 400°F, Gas Mark 6 for 10-12 minutes, until the pastry is crisp and golden.

*Serve with party drinks*

# EDIBLE PRESENTS

Home-made chocolates, biscuits and cookies, presented in attractive gift boxes,
make special gifts for your family and friends.

## SPICY GINGERBREAD STARS

*125 g (4 oz) liquid honey*
*125 g (4 oz) caster sugar*
*2 eggs*
*400 g (14 oz) plain flour*
*3 level teaspoons baking powder*
*1 teaspoon ground allspice*
*1 teaspoon ground ginger*
*icing sugar glaze*
*1 teaspoon mixed ground ginger and allspice*
*hundreds and thousands, or coloured caster sugar*

**1** Melt the honey in a saucepan over low heat, then allow to cool. Whisk in the sugar and eggs until frothy. Sift in the flour, baking powder and spices, a little at a time, and stir well. Shape into a soft dough and set aside to rest for 30-40 minutes.

**2** Roll out the dough to a thickness of 4 mm (¹/4 in) on a lightly floured surface. Cut into stars with a star-shaped cutter. Place them on greased baking sheets which have been lightly dusted with flour, leaving a little space between the stars. Bake in a preheated oven at 180°C, 350°F, Gas Mark 4 for 10-12 minutes.

**3** Cool on wire racks. Mix the icing sugar glaze with the mixed ginger and allspice, and ice the biscuits. Sprinkle with hundreds and thousands or coloured caster sugar.

*Makes: approximately 40 stars*

## FLORENTINES

*50 g (2 oz) unsalted butter*
*50 g (2 oz) caster sugar*
*25 g (1 oz) pistachio nuts, chopped*
*25 g (1 oz) walnuts, chopped*
*25 g (1 oz) flaked almonds*
*50 g (2 oz) candied peel, chopped*
*50 g (2 oz) glacé cherries, chopped*
*1 tablespoon double cream*
*75 g (3 oz) luxury plain chocolate, melted*
*75 g (3 oz) milk or white chocolate, melted*

**1** Melt the butter in a small saucepan. Stir in the sugar, bring to a fast boil and remove from the heat. Mix in the nuts, candied peel, cherries and cream.

**2** Line some baking trays with baking parchment and, using a teaspoon, drop small quantities of the mixture on to the trays. Bake in a preheated oven at 190°C, 375°F, Gas Mark 5 for 5-6 minutes. Leave to go cold on the trays.

**3** Spread a little melted chocolate on the back of each florentine and leave to set.

*Makes: approximately 30 Florentines*

# MINIATURE CHRISTMAS PUDDINGS

**For the pastry:**
100 g (3¹/2 oz) unsalted butter
175 g (6 oz) plain flour
25 g (1 oz) caster sugar
2-3 tablespoons cold water

**For the filling:**
450 g (1 lb) rich fruit cake, crumbled
3 tablespoons apricot jam
3 tablespoons dark rum

**For the decoration:**
icing sugar, for dusting
royal icing
marzipan (almond paste)
edible red and green food colourings

1 Make the pastry. Rub the butter into the flour until the mixture resembles fine breadcrumbs. Add the sugar and mix to a firm dough with the water. Roll out the pastry thinly on a lightly floured board and use to line about 30 x 5-cm (2-in) tartlet tins. Rest for 20 minutes.

2 Fill the pastry cases with a little foil and some baking beans. Bake in a preheated oven at 190°C, 375°F, Gas Mark 5 for 15 minutes. Cool and dust with icing sugar.

3 Meanwhile, make the filling. Mix the fruit cake crumbs with the apricot jam and rum, and shape into about 30 small balls. Place a ball in each pastry case.

4 Spread a little royal icing on each ball and leave to set. Colour a little marzipan green and shape into 30 holly leaves. Colour a little marzipan red and shape into 30 berries. Use to decorate the puddings.

*Makes: approximately 30 puddings*

# ANNA'S ALMOND MOONS

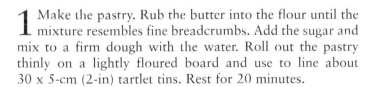

320 g (11 oz) vegetable shortening
140 g (5 oz) caster sugar
1 egg
600 g (1 lb 5 oz) plain flour
50 g (2 oz) roasted almonds, roughly chopped
icing sugar, for dusting

1 Cream the shortening with the sugar and then beat in the egg. Stir in the flour and almonds and mix together well to form a soft dough.

2 Divide the dough into 30 equal-sized pieces and shape each one into a 'moon'. Place on greased baking trays and bake in a preheated oven at 200°C, 400°F, Gas Mark 6 for 15-20 minutes.

3 Remove from the oven and allow to cool before dusting with icing sugar.

*Makes: approximately 30 moons*

# GRAND MARNIER TRUFFLES

My wife Sue makes these truffles for Christmas and ties them up in attractive little bags as presents for our family and friends.

*125 ml (4¹/₂ fl oz) double cream*
*50 g (2 oz) butter*
*600 g (1¹/₄ lb) good-quality milk chocolate*
*3 tablespoons brandy*
*50 ml (2 fl oz) Grand Marnier*
*115 g (4 oz) good-quality white chocolate*

**1** Bring the cream to the boil, add the butter and stir until it melts. Put 300 g (10 oz) of the milk chocolate in a bowl with the brandy and Grand Marnier. Stir in the hot cream and continue stirring until the chocolate melts and the mixture is smooth. Set aside to cool.

**2** Shape the chocolate mixture into small balls and place in the refrigerator until firm. Melt the remaining milk chocolate in a basin set over a pan of simmering water. Do the same with the white chocolate in another basin. Roll the chocolate shapes into balls and dip in the melted chocolate. Leave to set and then keep in the refrigerator.

*Makes: 60 truffles*

# MALAKOFF

Without doubt, these are the best chocolates I have ever had. Try them and see for yourself!

*100 g (3¹/₂ oz) whole hazelnuts, skinned*
*75 g (3 oz) sugar*
*100 g (3¹/₂ oz) good-quality white chocolate, melted*
*25 g (1 oz) peeled pistachios*
*115 g (4 oz) roasted flaked almonds*
*300 g (10 oz) good-quality milk chocolate*
*11 tablespoons hazelnut oil*

**1** Heat the hazelnuts in a preheated oven at 180°C, 350°F, Gas Mark 4. Put the sugar in a pan with 50 ml (2 fl oz) water and stir over low heat until completely dissolved. Bring to the boil and continue boiling until it turns a caramel colour. Remove from the heat, add the hot hazelnuts and bring back to the boil. Carefully add a little water and boil again to remove any lumpy crystals. Remove from the heat and cool until lukewarm.

**2** Liquidize the hazelnut caramel mixture to a paste and then stir into the melted white chocolate with the pistachios, almonds and oil. Melt 175 g (6 oz) of the milk chocolate in a basin placed over a pan of simmering water, and stir into the hazelnut chocolate mixture. Spread the mixture over the base of a 2.5-cm (1-in) deep tray and leave to set.

**3** When set, turn the chocolate over. Melt the remaining milk chocolate and spread over the top. Make decorative wavy lines over the surface with a comb-scraper and leave to set. Cut into 2.5-cm (1-in) long pieces to serve.

*Makes: approximately 20 chocolates*

# CHOCOLATE TUILE CORNETS

*100 g (3¹/₂ oz) icing sugar*
*100 g (3¹/₂ oz) plain flour*
*100 g (3¹/₂ oz) unsalted butter, melted and cooled*
*2 egg whites*
*1 teaspoon vanilla extract*
*2 teaspoons cocoa powder, sifted*
*2 teaspoons milk*

**For the filling:**
*100 g (3¹/₂ oz) luxury plain chocolate*
*120 ml ( 4 fl oz) double cream*

1 Sift the icing sugar and flour into a bowl. Quickly stir in the cooled butter, egg whites and vanilla extract to make a smooth paste. Reserve four tablespoons of this mixture. Mix the cocoa powder and milk together and add to the remaining mixture. Refrigerate for 30 minutes.

2 Drop 1¹/₂ teaspoons of the chocolate mixture in little heaps on baking trays lined with baking parchment. Spread out each heap to a round, 7.5 cm (3 in) in diameter. Using a small piping bag, fitted with a plain writing nozzle, pipe five lines of the reserved plain mixture across each chocolate round. With a skewer, draw lines across the piping in opposite directions to create a feathered effect.

3 Bake in a preheated oven at 190°C, 375°F, Gas Mark 5 for 4-5 minutes. Remove from the oven and quickly shape each biscuit around a cream horn tin or cylindrical mould. Leave to cool.

4 Make the filling. Place the chocolate and cream in a saucepan and heat gently until the chocolate melts. Remove from the heat and beat until smooth. Chill until firm and then beat again. Using a piping bag, fitted with a star nozzle, pipe a little filling into each cornet.

*Makes: approximately 20 cornets*

# GRANNY'S ALMOND COOKIES

*2 eggs*
*250 g (8 oz) sugar*
*1 level teaspoon allspice*
*75 g (3 oz) raisins*
*squeeze of lemon juice*
*250 g (8 oz) ground almonds*

1 Beat the eggs and sugar together until creamy. Add the allspice, raisins and lemon juice, and then mix in the ground almonds.

2 Using a teaspoon, drop small heaps of the mixture on to a baking tray lined with baking parchment, leaving some space between the heaps. Bake in a preheated oven at 180°C, 350°F, Gas Mark 4 for 15 minutes. Cool before storing in an airtight tin.

*Makes: approximately 25 cookies*

# TABLE DECORATIONS

To complement the festive food and drinks, you can decorate the table with some sumptuous flower arrangements utilizing seasonal foliage, classic candles and colourful flowers.

1 This candle arrangement will give your dinner table a romantic mood. The candles are looped with gold thread and set on a bed of evergreens and oystershell candles with a luxurious gold ribbon flounce. The cream and gold combine to create a simple but elegant look.

2 This richly coloured seasonal arrangement in a terracotta pot, which has been sprayed with gold and bronze paint, has a Baroque feel, with its dramatic wine red roses, tulips and carnations. Grapes, apples, lychees and mini-pineapples provide the finishing touches, and the crimson crushed velvet and gold cord add a touch of opulence.

3

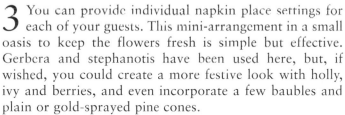

**3** You can provide individual napkin place settings for each of your guests. This mini-arrangement in a small oasis to keep the flowers fresh is simple but effective. Gerbera and stephanotis have been used here, but, if wished, you could create a more festive look with holly, ivy and berries, and even incorporate a few baubles and plain or gold-sprayed pine cones.

**4** This Christmas topiary tree looks stunning but is actually quite simple to make. All you need do is to stick a twisted piece of ivy root in a bed of moss in a terracotta pot and top it with an oasis ball enclosed in chicken wire. Cover it with seasonal green foliage such as fir, yew and cedar, then stud it with red roses or other flowers of your choice, small pineapples and other fruit, holly berries, gold-sprayed pine cones or ivy. To finish it off, use two loops of sweeping bear grass.

4

5 A traditional Advent wreath can make an attractive centrepiece for the table. We have used natural beeswax candles in an oasis ring of winter foliage, decorated with pine cones, grapes and tartan ribbons. If wished, you can add colour with holly berries, gold-sprayed pine cones and holly leaves, and cinnamon stick bundles, or use red or gold candles.

6 This opulent centrepiece for a large, very grand table is decorated with smart baubles, carnations, roses and fruits in a tray filled with oasis. Bear grass and seasonal evergreen foliage can be used to make a stunning decoration.

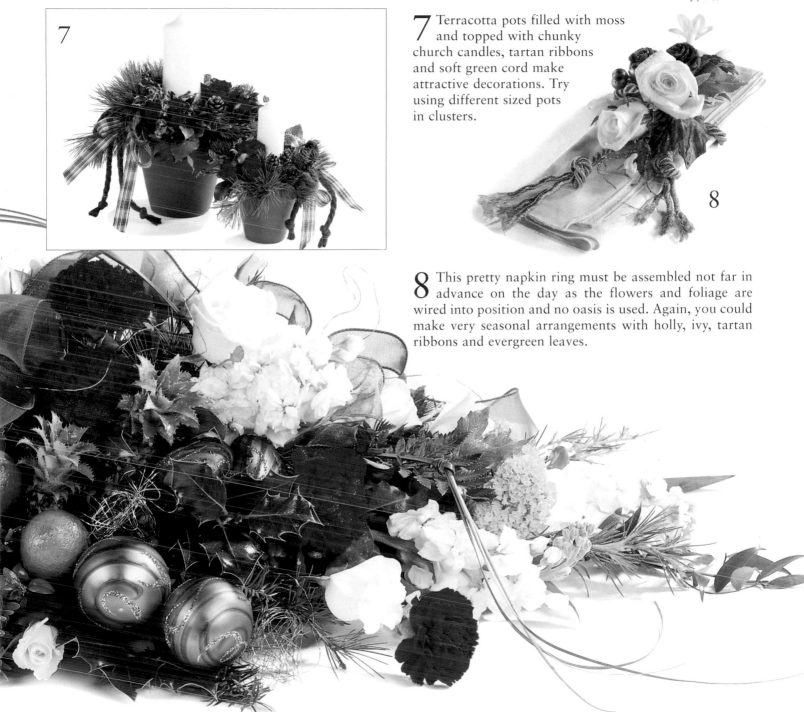

**7** Terracotta pots filled with moss and topped with chunky church candles, tartan ribbons and soft green cord make attractive decorations. Try using different sized pots in clusters.

**8** This pretty napkin ring must be assembled not far in advance on the day as the flowers and foliage are wired into position and no oasis is used. Again, you could make very seasonal arrangements with holly, ivy, tartan ribbons and evergreen leaves.

# CHRISTMAS TREE DECORATIONS

For most of us, bringing a fir tree into the home and decorating it is the first sign that Christmas really has begun. You can deck it out with shop-bought baubles and tinsel or make some yourself.

### 1 Choose a colour scheme

You can set the mood by choosing a colour scheme for both your Christmas tree decorations and the room itself. For example, you may opt for a traditional scheme of red and green with predominantly red baubles and candles for the tree, and garlands and wreaths of evergreen foliage and holly. Alternatively, you could choose a more opulent silver or gold and bedeck the tree with glittering silver or gold balls, bows, chains of beads and tinsel.

### 2 Make some decorations yourself

Children love making decorations and hanging them on the tree. In the weeks before Christmas, you can have fun making painted cut-out stars sprinkled with glitter; festive bows in silver, gold or tartan ribbon; metallic paper chains to swirl around the tree and thread through the branches; and pine cones sprayed silver or gold.

### 3 Home-baked tree decorations

Your children might like to make some gingerbread men and stars to decorate the tree. Decorate them with glacé icing and silver balls and use gold thread to hang them on the tree. Baked cookies can be cut into stars, hearts or Christmas tree shapes and then covered with gold or silver foil.

### 4 The finishing touches

A beautifully dressed tree needs an attractive tub in which to stand. If you use an old bucket or earthenware pot, don't forget to cover it with brightly coloured wrapping paper or spray it with gold, silver or bronze paint. Real candles in tiny candle holders add the best finishing touch of all and cast a soft, mellow light which is more subtle and traditional than electric 'fairy lights'. However, take care and don't leave the tree unattended while the candles are lit.

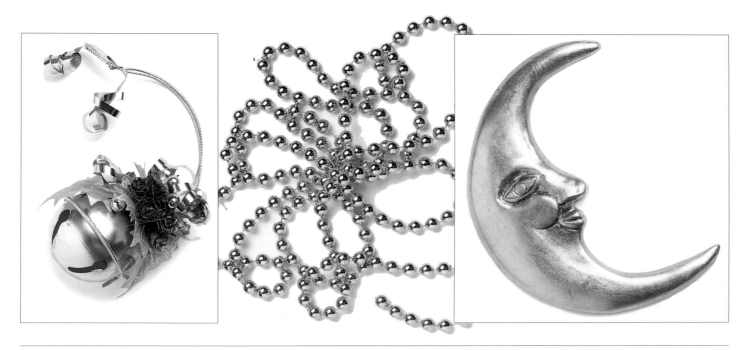

# CHRISTMAS PARTY GAMES

The tradition of the family sitting down together and playing games at Christmas dates back to the parlour games of the nineteenth century. Most of still enjoy switching off the television set and playing some entertaining games. Board games are very popular but it is often more fun to be creative and inventive in your approach. Inhibitions and reserve are swept away as relatives, friends and guests all enter into the spirit of the occasion. Here is a selection of games for you to try. Have fun!

## CHARADES

This ageless parlour game is still one of the all-time favourites. You will need two teams, each of which chooses a two-or three-syllable word which they act out and the other side has to guess. The word is acted out, syllable by syllable, accompanied by mime. For example, 'mistletoe' could be split into 'miss', 'Al' and 'toe'. It could be a seasonal word or the name of a book, a play, a film etc.

## CONSEQUENCES

Most of us have played this at some time or other. Its charm is that you don't have to keep it tame but can make it as rude and funny as you like. Everyone is given a pencil and paper, writes down the name of a male character to start the game off, folds the paper in half and passes it on to the player sitting beside him who then writes down the name of a female character, folds it over and passes it on again, and so the game continues. The set formula is as follows:

- Male character meets
- Female character
- Where they met
- What he did
- What she did
- What he said
- What she said
- And the consequence was...
- And the world said...

When the pieces of paper are unfolded at the end and the story read out, it can be very amusing.

**Note:** you can do a variation on this theme by drawing

pictures of animals, people, things etc., starting from the top and working downwards, and folding the paper over and passing it on between the head and neck etc.

## DICTIONARY GAME

Better known as the television panel game Call My Bluff, everyone divides into two teams and each team picks an obscure word, looking it up in a dictionary. One person gives the correct definition while the other members of the team make up false definitions. The members of the other team have to guess the correct definition and who is telling the truth.

## SARDINES

If you are feeling more energetic and adventurous, then sardines may be the game for you. Children and teenagers love it but you're never too old to play. One person is sent off to hide and then the lights are switched off in the house and the other players have to find him. Each player who finds him joins him in his hiding place, and the last player to find him has to be the next person to hide.

## MUSICAL CUSHIONS

This is musical chairs with cushions. Place the cushions on the floor in a line in the centre of the room with one less cushion than there are players. Music is played and the players dance round the cushions. When the music is stopped, each player has to find a spare cushion to sit down on – the player who can't find one drops out and another cushion is removed, and so forth until only one player is left.

# INDEX